Performance Management
in Education

Published in Association with the British Educational Leadership and Management Association

This series of books published for BELMAS aims to be directly relevant to the concerns and professional development needs of emergent leaders and experienced leaders in schools. The series editors are Professor Harry Tomlinson, and Dr Hugh Busher, School of Education, University of Leicester.

Titles include:

Performance Management in Education: Improving Practice (2002)
By Jenny Reeves, Christine Forde, Jim O'Brien, Pauline Smith and Harry Tomlinson

Strategic Management for School Development: Leading your school's improvement strategy (2002)
By Brian Fidler

Subject Leadership and School Improvement (2000)
By Hugh Busher and Alma Harris with Christine Wise

School Improvement After Inspection? School and LEA responses Edited by Peter Earley

Living Headship: voices, values and vision (1999)
Edited by Harry Tomlinson

School Culture (1999)
Edited by Jon Prosser

Policy, Leadership and Professional Knowledge in Education (1998)
Edited by Michael Strain, Bill Dennison, Janet Ousten and Valerie Hall

Managing Continuous Professional Development in Schools (1997)
Edited by Harry Tomlinson

Choices for Self-managing schools: autonomy and accountability (1997)
Edited by Brian Fidler

Performance Management in Education

Improving Practice

Jenny Reeves, Christine Forde,
Jim O'Brien, Pauline Smith
and Harry Tomlinson

P·C·P
Paul Chapman
Publishing

Paul Chapman Publishing
A SAGE Publications Company
6 Bonhill Street
London EC2A 4PU

SAGE Publications Inc
2455 Teller Road
Thousand Oaks, California 91320

SAGE Publications India Pvt Ltd
32, M-Block Market
Greater Kailash – I
New Delhi 1 10 048

Library of Congress Control Number 2001135922

A catalogue record of this book is available from the British Library

ISBN 0 7619 7171 8
ISBN 0 7619 7172 6

Library of Congress catalogue record available

Typeset by Annesett, Weston-super-Mare, North Somerset
Printed and bound in Great Britain by Athenaeum Press, Tyne and Wear

Contents

Series Editor's Preface   vi

Preface   ix

Acknowledgements   xi

List of contributors   xii

List of abbreviations   xiv

1   An introduction to performance management and improving practice   1

2   The concern with performance and continuing professional development   16

3   Changing rewards: performance-related pay   39

4   Changing professional practice   56

5   Work-based learning   79

6   Building capability for work-based learning   100

7   Improving performance: the learners' view   124

8   Assessing performance   147

9   Achieving improvement: developing policy and practice in schools   169

References   177

Index   187

Series Editor's Preface

This exciting and timely book explores the development and developing understandings of performance in England and Wales and Scotland. This use of two of the administrative units within the British Isles allows authors and readers to draw comparison between two different approaches to education – the Scottish system of education has been independent of that of England and Wales for many years. In doing so they raise a critical debate about central government and other authorities search for `best practice' models that will somehow be able to fit all situations and locations, by pointing out that successful practice may take many forms depending on what values policy-makers privilege. They also importantly argue that performance management need not necessarily be linked to pay and point out how Scottish and English and Welsh policy diverge on this issue.

Early in the book the authors acknowledge the differences of approach between managerial and professional perspectives on performance management. They make it clear that although they understand the values that have driven the introduction of managerialist perspectives of performance management to education, they consider that professional approaches allow for equal rigour of accountability and have the advantage of encouraging teachers to be personally professionally engaged with constantly monitoring their standards of work. In this testing regime of action learning they perceive mentors having a key role in supporting teachers and helping them review critically their working practices.

The book focuses on what is essentially a modernist project, rather than a post modern or post structural one. The authors focus on the growth of social structures to promote professional development, pointing out how difficult it is for teachers to sustain personal development if there is insufficient formal and informal support for it. Helpfully, one chapter traces the development of Continuing Professional Development (CPD) provision in England and Wales and Scotland, setting an important policy context in which, and sometimes against which, teachers have struggled to improve the quality of their performance. It leads the authors into a discussion of the importance of competence-based or standards-based approaches to defining teacher performance. While they acknowledge that such approaches risk being narrow and behaviourist they indicate how they can be broadened to incorporate understandings of values and indicate that such approaches can bring greater coherence to planning and managing the improvement of teachers' performance. So do views that teachers can successfully and rigorously exercise control of their professional practices and development elide noiselessly into concern for the effective if subtle management or control of teachers through `soft' human resources development, a system that, of course, stands in contradiction to professional autonomy.

However, the modernist project of performance management is attenuated, as the authors acknowledge. They note the recent renewed interest in and sponsorship by the English and Welsh central government of teachers' engagement in research to explore good practice in schools, and argue that it is further emphasis on work-based learning that is the key to the full potential value of CPD for teachers. If the parameters against which to make judgements of what constitutes good practice for teachers, and senior and middle level leaders and managers in schools too, are now set by central government through its agencies, the processes of collecting evidence of practice rigorously through observation and other methods, giving feedback by observer to practitioner, and discussion of performance and how to improve it allows teachers of all qualities at a local level to re-assert professional control over their development. It is how practitioners make sense of their experiences and engage with professionally held and developed understandings of effective practice, including processes of change and the modifications in practice that they implement, that ultimately leads to sustained change, whatever intrinsic and extrinsic motivation spurs them to undertake professional development in the first place.

As well as reviewing the key issues and concepts underpinning the tensions inherent in successful professional development, the authors also set out a clear programme for implementing effective performance management, while noting that the transplantation of practice from commercial sector businesses to public sector services is neither straightforward nor as easy to achieve successfully as is sometimes naively proclaimed. Nonetheless they argue the importance of trying to manage teacher professional development successfully to improve students' opportunities for learning. To achieve this, they suggest senior and middle leaders in schools need to foster a culture of learning, amongst staff as well as among students, and build teachers' capacity to carry out effective professional development. The professional development itself needs to focus actively and rigorously on the evaluation and improvement of practice. However, unless the social and organisational systems in schools and local authorities, and central government policy and funding also enable such approaches to performance management these will not be successful.

So the book moves back and forth, as a successful book on education leadership and management should, between the macro external policy contexts and the micro internal organisational processes of leadership, management and practice and reflections on practice by individual practitioners, showing how these different levels of action and sense making by participants in the action are interconnected. The success of teacher professional development cannot be divorced from its organisational contexts, and the impact of performance management has to be understood in both its policy contexts and those of the individual practitioners' perceptions of it. Similarly the purposes of performance management through professional development have to be understood within two frameworks, that of control and accountability – ensuring that teachers and school leaders perform adequately to support effective and inclusive student learning, and that of adaptability – empowering school leaders and teachers to respond flexibly to changing situations and students' needs while maintaining successful approaches to effective learning.

Hugh Busher,
University of Leicester,
School of Education

Preface

This book has grown from research and development work associated with the design and implementation of the Scottish Qualification for Headship (SQH). The development of this national professional qualification for those aspiring to headship in Scotland was funded by the SOEID (Scottish Office Education and Industry Department). Throughout the development of the qualification those involved have grappled with the issue of how to provide a programme of development that would enable those candidates pursuing it to acquire and demonstrate sound practice in school leadership and management.

Within the current political climate that demands schools demonstrate continual improvement, there is an increasing emphasis on enhancing the quality of the work of teachers and school leaders. Resulting interventions to support performance management raise questions about what it means to be a teacher, a school manager, a professional and, ultimately, about the nature of schools themselves.

The improvement of performance is a more complex and demanding process than some simplistic performance management models would suggest. Key to improvement is the developmental process, and staff development (CPD) is now seen as a major strategic tool in building the capability of staff to deliver a curriculum that supports the achievement of all pupils. However, what form this staff development should take is problematic. There is often a lack of clarity on the part of those who commission and provide professional development opportunities as to both the purposes and the processes of teacher learning. What this book seeks to explore is how CPD can have a positive impact on the performance of individual staff members within a school.

We begin by considering the increasing political emphasis on performance management in the public services and outline the current policy position in the UK in relation to teachers, including performance-related and progression-related pay. In presenting these current initiatives, however, we take a critical stance. The major thrust of the book is to explore work-based learning as a pivotal component in any developmental initiative that seeks to improve performance. Our object is to conceptualise the process of work-based learning and to consider the implications this has for establishing and using these methodologies to support the development of practice in schools. We then use our own and others' experience of the implementation of the Scottish Qualification for Headship (SQH) to exemplify the preceding discussions.

Jenny Reeves, Christine Forde,
Jim O'Brien, Pauline Smith
and Harry Tomlinson

Acknowledgements

This book would not have been possible if it had not been for the work, energy and enthusiasm of all those involved in the pilot and launch of the SQH programme, particularly the candidates on the standard and accelerated routes, the local authority co-ordinators, tutors and field assessors. The many hours of debate and reflection that were part of the piloting process helped in shaping the ideas we have explored in this book.

The authors would also like to thank SEED (Scottish Executive Education Department) for their support of the project and Viv Casteel, who shared the task of leading the project as national development officer.

List of contributors

Jim O'Brien is Vice Dean of the Faculty of Education in the University of Edinburgh. He has been a teacher, lecturer in guidance and pastoral care, and director of In-Service with responsibility for teacher CPD. He has contributed to several national development programmes in Scotland including appraisal and review, the Scottish Qualification for Headship and currently the development of the Standard for Chartered Teacher. He has published in the fields of CPD, leadership and management and school improvement. A current focus is on multi-media CPD resources for teachers and he has co-authored a number of CDRoms including *Dealing with Disruption* (SEED, 2001); *Issues in School Improvement* (Hong Kong Department of Education, 2002); *Raising the Standard: Study Support* (Prince's Trust, 1999).

Pauline Smith is a senior education adviser with the DfES, working in the Standards and Effectiveness Unit and Teachers' Professional Development division. She worked previously at the Crewe School of Education, Manchester Metropolitan University, where she was head of CPD, managing large-scale modular inservice programmes for teachers and lecturing in education management at postgraduate level. Pauline has also worked for the OU for the past ten years and is an experienced external examiner of English, Welsh and Scottish education management programmes, including the SQH. She has also worked as a LEA adviser, NPQH lead assessor, OFSTED inspector and performance management consultant developing a keen interest in the management of school-based training and assessment. Pauline has published in the fields of mentoring, CPD, leadership and management; recent publications include *Living Headship* with Tomlinson and Gunter.

Harry Tomlinson is a professor at Leeds Metropolitan University where he was responsible for the MBA in Educational Leadership. He is Centre Manager for the Yorkshire and Humber Region for two major contracts, the National Professional Qualification for Headship (NPQH) for the National College for School Leadership (NCSL) and Performance Management for the DfES. He is also Project Director for one of the seven consortia delivering the Leadership Programme for

Serving Headteachers (LPSH) for the NCSL. After 18 years in secondary headship his main interests are school leadership and school performance as evidenced in books *Performance Related Pay in Education, The Search for Standards, Managing Continuing Professional Development in Schools,* and , with Helen Gunter and Pauline Smith *'Living Headship: Voices, Values and Vision'.*

Christine Forde is Head of the Department of Educational Studies in the Faculty of Education at Glasgow University. She is the SQH Pro- gramme Co-ordinator within the faculty and was involved in the piloting of the SQH as an author and tutor. She has worked in teacher education for a number of years specialising initially in primary edu- cation and, more recently, in educational leadership and management and the continuing development of teachers. She has worked as a local authority adviser as a member of the Staff College team in Strathclyde Regional Council and as a primary teacher. Her recent publications have been concerned with the development of the Scottish Qualifica- tion for Headship and with the area of teacher education.

Jenny Reeves is Director of Continuing Professional Development at the Institute of Education at the University of Stirling. From 1997 to 2000 she worked with Viv Casteel as National Development Officer for the Scottish Qualification for Headship. Prior to this she was involved in designing and delivering management development as a member of Staff College team for Strathclyde Regional Council. Her publications include a series of articles on the development and impact of the Scottish Qualification for Headship that focuses on work-based approaches to management development for aspiring headteachers and other work on headteacher development, including chapters in MacBeath, J. (ed.) (1998) *Effective School Leadership: Responding to Change.*

List of abbreviations

CCSS	Council of Chief State School Officers
CERI	Centre for Educational Research and Innovation
CPD	continuing professional development
CPRE	Consortium for Policy Research in Education
CT	Chartered Teacher
DfEE	Department for Education and Employment
EAZ	Education Action Zone
EIC	Excellence in Cities
ERA	Education Reform Act 1988
ETS	Educational Testing Service
GRIDS	Guidelines for Review and Internal Development
GTC	General Teaching Council
HEI	higher education institute
HRM	human resources management
ICT	information communication technology
IIE	Industry in Education
ILEA	Inner London Education Authority
INSET	in-service education and training
INTASC	Interstate New Teacher Assessment and Support Consortium
IPD	Institute of Personnel and Development
ISIP	International School Improvement Project
ITE	initial teacher education
LEA	local education authority
LPSH	Leadership Programme for Serving Headteachers
NBPTS	National Board for Professional Teaching Standards
NCITT	National Committee on the In-service Training of Teachers
NCSL	National College for School Leadership
NPQH	National Professional Qualification for Headship
NQT	newly qualified teacher
OD	organisational development
OECD	Organisation for Economic Co-operation and Development
OfSTED	Office for Standards in Education
PRP	performance-related pay
QTS	Qualified Teacher Status
SBPA	School-Based Performance Awards
SEED	Scottish Executive Education Department
SHS	Standard for Headship
SMT	senior management team
SOEID	Scottish Office Education and Industry Department
SQH	Scottish Qualification for Headship
STRB	School Teachers Review Body
TEI	teacher education institute
TQM	total quality management
TTA	Teacher Training Agency
WBL	work-based learning

1

An introduction to performance management and improving practice

This book has been written at a time when the issue of improving teacher effectiveness is at the very centre of policy development in the field of education. In the UK we are experiencing the rapid implementation of a raft of initiatives to restructure the way in which the work of both schools and particularly teachers is defined and managed. Occupational standards for teachers, a National Curriculum for initial teacher training, frameworks for career development and continuing professional development (CPD), the re-launching of appraisal, evidence-based assessment of performance and performance-related pay (PRP) are part of this current drive to achieve the 'modernisation' of the education service in England and Wales. In Scotland, too, similar developments are underway under the aegis of the newly formed Scottish Executive.

Finding a place to stand in the middle of this storm of activity is quite daunting but very necessary because the risks involved in this headlong rush to reform and restructure are considerable given the very real questions about the purpose and nature of education raised by current social, economic, political, technological and ecological changes. In such an unpredictable environment, making the right choices becomes increasingly difficult, as has been underlined by the recent riots in Bradford and Oldham. The government's commitment to encouraging increasing diversity in the choice of schooling for various groups was seriously called into question by these events, particularly given the findings of the inquiry into the school system in Bradford, chaired by Herman Ouseley in 2001, which had identified a racially segregated schooling system as a cause for concern.

We do not pretend to have any answers to these issues but we do want to make a contribution to the debate about performance management based on our experience of working with teachers and school managers in the UK over a number of years in developing work-based learning programmes designed to improve performance. Thus our particular focus is on professional development within the context of performance management. There are two particular issues we want to explore. The first of these, in line with the commitment in *A Strategy for Professional Development* (DfEE, 2001b) to investigate the impact of CPD, is to explore what it means to alter or improve performance; the second is to argue for an approach to performance management that fixes on the longer term and the need for the teaching profession to be able to respond to ongoing change rather than to conform to a set of teaching prescriptions based on the here and now. For us the kind of reliance on the precepts and practices of human resource management inherent in current policy is worrying. To lapse into the purely anecdotal it is worth remembering that an avowedly excellent performance management system did not save a leading British retailer from becoming ineffectual. Management practices cannot serve as ends in themselves, they need to be shaped and modified in the light of purposes and needs.

Of course, improving performance can be viewed crudely as 'getting them to pull their socks up' on the assumption that with good control mechanisms and sufficient pressure staff will perform better. While this approach may bring about dramatic changes under certain circumstances, it leads only to limited short-term improvements because it is essentially non-developmental and it is predicated on a very narrow definition of what the nature of the 'performance problem' is. Given the demands placed on the education system through successive waves of reform and restructuring and the continuing need to respond to change, we believe the 'problem' of performance is far more complex than a matter of ensuring conformity to a series of performance indicators.

We shall touch on some of these complexities in the course of our discussion but our major theme is that worthwhile and sustained improvement is only achievable through a process of learning in a supportive environment. Our core concern in this book is the developmental aspect of performance management. We hope our insights into this process will help to inform the choices of some of our readers, whether based in schools or other branches of the education service.

Whilst we will be concentrating on individual performance this will be continually set in the context of the school because, as we shall argue, we do not see the individual performance of teachers and the organisational context in which they work as separable. Although we are looking at issues of development for individuals, we also feel it is important to remember, as Deming (1982) and Juran (1989) constantly reminded managers in industry, that most performance problems are due to faulty systems and processes within organisations rather than to individuals.

In this chapter we shall concentrate on defining some of the key concepts pertinent to our main discussion of the parameters for improving professional practice, in particular 'performance management', 'performance' and 'improvement'.

Defining performance management

Within the education service, as in other public services, performance management is a contentious issue (Bottery, 2000). Underlying the debate is the question of the role and status of teachers. The contrast is made between treating teachers as technicians, whose role is to carry out prescribed tasks, or as professionals, who are trusted to develop practice appropriate to the learners in their care. This could be dismissed as merely being an argument about vested interest with teachers and educationalists fighting to retain professional autonomy, but it touches on two more fundamental issues:

1) What will be required of teachers in the future? Will they become technicians responding consistently within a fairly limited range of practice or will they need the capability to act flexibly and responsively across an increasingly complex field?
2) What kind of organisations should schools be and what values and principles should underpin relationships in institutions which provide education?

In making practical decisions about how improvement of performance should be approached in schools these issues can be seen as fundamental in determining decisions about policy and implementation.

There are a number of ways of defining performance management:

1) As a particular set of practices implemented by managers and aimed at influencing the behaviours and the outcomes achieved by individuals in organisations.
2) As a range of managerial techniques aimed at influencing the outcomes achieved by groups and individuals at both organisational level and across groups of organisations.
3) As an approach to improving their own practice used by individuals and groups.

Broadly 1) and 2) are characteristic of a managerial approach to improving performance whilst 3) is generally regarded as consistent with an approach to improvement advocated in professional settings. As our discussion will indicate, despite the polarisation of the debate, the division in terms of practice remains mixed both in education and the commercial field.

Managerial approaches

For many people, performance management is defined by a very specific set of practices developed to control the behaviour of individuals in commercial organisations. Through formal appraisal systems and PRP, organisations seek to ensure their employees are motivated to work hard and effectively. Goal-setting theory (Locke, 1997) provides much of the underpinning logic for the practice in that people are to be motivated by working towards challenging but attainable goals they regard as worth while. The DfEE's guidelines *Performance Management in Schools* (2000b: 5) provide a typical example of this formulation. The document (*ibid.*) defines performance management as 'an on-going cycle, not an event' consisting of three annual stages:

1) *Planning* – discussion and recording of priorities and objectives and how progress will be monitored.
2) *Monitoring* – constant review of progress providing support if necessary.
3) *Review* – evaluation of the teacher's performance taking account of progress against objectives.

The thorny process of assigning pay on the basis of review is confined to an annex.

During training for managers, the appraisal cycle has often been represented in this manner as a discrete set of activities divorced from other means of improving organisational performance. More generally, however, it is seen as part of a more elaborate system, as suggested by Armstrong and Baron (1998: 7): 'Performance management is a strategic and integrated approach to delivering sustained success to organisations by improving the performance of people who work in them and by developing the capabilities of teams and individual contributors.'

The characteristics of an organisation that practises performance management are that it:

- communicates a vision of its objectives to all its employees;
- sets departmental and individual performance targets that are related to wider objectives;
- conducts a formal review process to identify training, development and reward outcomes; and
- evaluates the whole process in order to improve effectiveness.

In addition, 'performance management organisations':

- express performance targets in terms of measurable outputs, accountabilities and training/learning targets;
- use formal appraisal procedures as ways of communicating performance requirements which are set on a regular basis;
- link performance requirements to pay, especially for senior managers (*ibid.*: 45).

This more systemic approach to performance management is often further elaborated to provide a set of complex procedures that, for example, within the schools sector, operate at the levels of the individual teacher, the school and the local authority:

> In virtually all sectors, operational decentralisation has been accompanied by the extended development of performance management systems. Such systems seemed designed both to monitor and shape organisational behaviour and encompass a range of techniques including performance review, staff appraisal systems, performance-related pay, scrutinies, so-called quality audits, customer feedback mechanisms, comparative table of performance indicators including 'league tables', charter marks, customer charters, quality standards and total quality management (Hoggett, quoted in Mahony and Hextall, 2000: 32).

A professional approach

These managerial systems for performance management are often contrasted with the professional model where the management of performance is seen as the responsibility of the individual professional. Hoyle and John (1995) suggest that ideas about professionals being autonomous sit alongside ideas about responsibility. Implicit in this notion of professionality is a sense of duty to perform to a level necessary to ensure the well-being of the client. By simply 'being a professional' a person understands and acts upon the obligation to carry out the tasks effectively for the benefit of the client.

Eraut (1994) identifies a number of aspects in the accountability of the individual professional, clearly indicating that it is now an essential attribute of professionalism. The issue of providing an appropriate service is still strong within this approach ('a moral commitment to serve the interests of clients'), but equally strong is a self-directed process of ongoing development and performance enhancement: 'a professional obligation to self-monitor and to periodically review the effectiveness of one's practice; a professional obligation to expand one's repertoire, to reflect on one's experience and to develop one's expertise' (*ibid*.: 236).

This model has a major drawback from an accountability perspective in that the obligation to self-evaluate is not open to scrutiny and, therefore, whilst some professionals might put this at the centre of their practice, others might not. However, Eraut's fourth and fifth items ('an obligation that is professional as well as contractual to contribute to the quality of one's organisation' and 'an obligation to reflect upon and contribute to discussions about the changing role of one's profession in wider society' – *ibid*.) provide a basis for professionals to render account to others.

We can conveniently contrast the two approaches by placing them at the extremes of performance management as constructs at the 'hard' and the 'soft' end of a continuum. The differences between these two positions centre on issues of responsibility and relationships and they are expressed through different forms of practice (see Table 1.1).

But is this dichotomy as secure as it looks? The more widespread adoption of the notions of reflective practice within a number of sectors, partly under the banner of total quality management (TQM), demonstrates a growing congruence between managerialist and professional approaches with an emphasis on self-evaluation, growth and participation, 'democratic' decision-making and shared values. Indeed the approach has even extended into classrooms where many teachers are increasingly involved in a 'performance management cycle' in their work with young people – negotiating targets and

Table 1.1   Contrastive approaches to maintaining and improving performance

Line management hierarchy	Individual autonomy
Establishes systems of control:	Sense of duty pervades:
• Policies.	• Obligations.
• Codes of practice.	• Self-regulation in interests of client.
• Performance criteria, standards.	• Maintain and enhance expertise.
• Formal appraisal.	• Self-monitoring of performance.

acting as mentors and coaches as part of raising attainment and fostering independent learning. As Bottery (2000: 94) points out:

> TQM appears to provide individuals with more motivation, more involvement, more control over their work. Furthermore, the concept of the internal customer indicates that internal hierarchies, should where necessary be turned upside down in order to empower front-line individuals, or at the very least to permit them to work out the best way of serving their 'customers'.

It could be argued therefore that TQM is potentially subversive of the managerial agenda and its use in schools could be supportive of increasing the power and decision-making role of those who are in the front line of serving children and young people allowing them to challenge and overturn central directives. Maybe, as Bottery intimates, this accounts for its lack of popularity with policy-makers – the adoption of such initiatives as Investors in People and the European Foundation for Quality Management has been supported because they have not so far threatened the supremacy of inspection as the major strategy for quality control.

This parallel between TQM and professional models creates unease in some quarters. As the description of the practices of the two approaches becomes more congruent, some educationalists feel that acceptance of personal responsibility and the obligation to self-monitor could be used manipulatively to undermine allegiance to a public service ethic. These elements of the professional model could be used to promote a rather different set of values at odds with practice based on a moral purpose for education (Hartley, 1997).

Defining performance

The professions have always had a concern with performance and the maintenance of standards by practitioners even if this was largely motivated by a desire to ensure that only members of professional bodies were seen as competent and employable. Initially, competence to practise was defined in intellectual terms and established by the use of qualifying examinations (Eraut, 1994). This remains as a key feature of entry into many of the professions.

Once someone enters work there are basically two approaches to assessing the quality of his or her performance. The first concentrates on the outcomes he or she achieves and the second on the behaviours he or she displays, and this is expressed in performance management systems through using different sets of performance measures:

- setting goals and targets defined in quantifiable terms which the individual or group must achieve; and
- delineating specific and observable sets of behaviours to be displayed.

The next obvious and logical step is to combine these two measures by specifying the behaviours that lead to positive outcomes to create a means both for assessing performance and arriving at a basis for improving it.

There is a body of work, originating largely in the USA but increasingly popular in the UK since the 1980s, that seeks to define what constitutes competent performance and to use the resultant frameworks as a basis for staff development (Esp, 1993). Despite the increasing use of such performance measures in the field of education, many have voiced strong opposition to these initiatives. Professional practice is regarded as too varied and context specific to make such a detailed approach to specifying behaviour either useful or desirable (Barnett, 1994). Areas of professional action are not so easily defined because they are shaped by:

- context
- clients' needs
- accumulated knowledge
- experience
- judgement.

Additionally, what constitutes competent performance for any given profession depends more upon current opinions about what makes for a good practitioner and the circumstances under which such practitioners are expected to operate than any ultimate 'scientific' yardstick for performance. For instance, in teaching a particular mode of engaging the learner may be more or less effective depending on the context in which the teaching takes place. A technique that works very well on a one-to-one basis may well be ineffective when applied to a group of 30 learners. Any current basis of judgement (for example, the TTA Teaching Standards or OfSTED ratings as to what makes for effective teaching) is based upon a set of cultural assumptions about schooling and appropriate forms of provision for the education of young people. Thus in addition to the general questions about what constitutes good performance we have to remember this can never be defined in wholly objective or absolute terms. The characteristics of the good schoolteacher are dependent on changing definitions of education, schooling and teaching and learning.

The criticism of the use of competences (behaviours derived from functional analyses) has led to a slight broadening of definitions. In a recent survey of current practice in relation to performance management in industry, Armstrong and Baron (1998: 8–9) saw performance management as being concerned with:

Outputs – the achievement of results
Outcomes – the impact on overall performance of this achievement
Competencies – the processes required to achieve these results
Capabilities – the inputs in terms of knowledge, skill and competence.

There have also been compromises made in the public services to make competences compatible with a public service ethic through the inclusion of values in competence frameworks. Perhaps the best known of these are the ASSET (Winter and Maisch, 1996) standards in social work. In higher education the use of the term 'capability' to cover both behavioural and conceptual aspects of practice represents another approach to reconciliation.

However, it is worth remembering that standards did not always have the demonised status that is currently so prevalent in the academic literature. At one time, as Mahony and Hextall (2000) remind us, they were seen as a means of promoting social justice. The profile of 'criteria for good practice' for student teachers developed at a London teacher training college in the 1980s was motivated by a progressive attempt to promote equal opportunities. The profile was intended to be transparent (and therefore open to challenge); inclusive in its development of an account of good practice; supportive of student teachers' professional development by enabling them to participate in negotiating the agenda for their learning; open about the basis on which students would be assessed; more widely accountable; and responsive within a public education system (*ibid.*: 31). Mahony and Hextall go on to make a useful distinction between a regulatory approach and a developmental approach to the design and use of standards which assigns them with a very different significance and meaning. It is encouraging that the recently relaunched National Standards Framework for Teachers in England (DfEE, 2001b) shows a greater commitment to their formative and developmental use. The framework is described as being 'entirely voluntary' and as a means of enabling teachers and those who work with them to identify learning needs. None the less, we would question whether their continued avoidance of the need for examining values and purposes and therefore being supportive of critical reflection makes them as valuable as they might be.

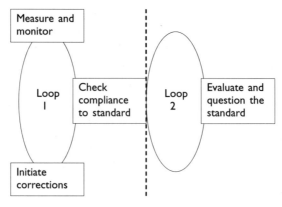

Figure 1.1 Single and double-loop learning
Source: Adapted from Baguley (1994: 19)

Defining improvement

Improvement is also a key term in our discussion and it is important to be clear about what kind of improvement is being referred to as the subject of performance management. The meanings that currently attach to the word in organisational settings can be roughly divided between understanding improvement as:

- increasing efficiency and reliability; or
- developing the ability to respond and adapt to changing circumstances.

These two definitions are not exclusive, and Argyris and Schon's (1974) notion of single-loop and double-loop learning (see Figure 1.1) is helpful in pointing to both to the differences between these two sets of assumptions and to their relationship.

Single-loop improvement

Underpinning this form of improvement is the assumption that what should be done is well known and therefore the performance problem is to make sure it is happening. This definition of improvement assumes there are no real problems with goals and purposes and that what matters are results. The key to improvement is conformity in achieving predetermined objectives and standards (see Table 1.2).

The focus of this form of improvement tends to be remedial and has been heavily endorsed and 'rewarded' by inspection systems in the public services (Rogers, 1999).

Table 1.2   Effects of single-loop learning

Efficiency	Maintaining the same standard of service for less input or raising output measures for the same level of resource.
Reliability	Ensuring the same standard of service from all units for the same input.

When systems of monitoring show that people are not acting according to specification, the logic is that adjustments in performance have to be made. Arguably, this strategy becomes more 'aspirational' with benchmarking that is fixing desired outcomes at the level achieved through best practice in comparable organisations. The more negative aspect of the process is where it is fuelled by the desire to get a quart out of a pint pot through setting higher and higher targets without increasing, or even whilst reducing, available resources.

Double-loop improvement

Here there is less certainty about the future. This definition of improvement assumes that goals and purposes as well as results must be constantly monitored so the performance problem is not simply one of conformity but of having the capacity to respond appropriately to change. For instance, it might be argued that both the ends and the means of educating children and young people are changing and therefore improvement consists in both responding appropriately to these changes and in becoming more adaptable and flexible (see Table 1.3). Double-loop improvement does not preclude concerns with efficiency and reliability but it goes beyond these boundaries and requires a rather different set of attitudes and capabilities than those needed for single-loop improvement.

Problems can clearly arise when there is a muddling of these two approaches. For instance, in the case of disciplinary problems in school, a single-loop approach would look to re-jigging discipline pol-

Table 1.3   Effects of double-loop learning

Effectiveness	Changing the nature of the service to meet new needs.
Adaptability	Increasing the capacity and capability of the organisation to provide services that meet changing needs and circumstances.

icy and tightening procedures, whereas a double-loop approach might seek to question the staff's and parents' assumptions about school discipline and explore new ways of engaging pupils.

Determining the nature of the performance problem

The growing pressure on teacher performance is in itself a symptom of a restructuring of the whole sector that continues to gather pace. In this book we view the 'problem' of performance as one of responding to substantive change. We do not believe, despite media rhetoric, that the teaching forces of the western world all suffered a disastrous and simultaneous loss of competence because of a sudden change in teachers' personal characteristics and their adoption of misguided notions of what education was about. Rather we believe that any 'loss of competence' was the outcome of the restructuring of the education service and the major economic, technological and social changes that have taken, and continue to take, place. Teachers and headteachers are now expected to perform a substantially different role from that performed even ten years ago.

The causes of these changes in role are both ideological and practical. They have been driven partly by a particular set of beliefs about the role of the state and the public services (Clarke and Newman, 1997; Bottery, 2000) and partly by changes in the social context that have substantially altered attitudes, expectations and relationships in the schools sector (Levin and Riffel, 1997).

Whilst single-loop improvement will always be an issue in schools, as it is for most organisations, we believe the main performance problem facing teachers and schools is going to be coping with double-loop improvement. On this basis we believe that learning how to learn and developing the capacity to adapt, work jointly with others and be both inventive and prepared to take risks are appropriate goals for improvement in performance in the education service in the longer term.

Selecting the means for improvement

The major battleground in performance improvement lies between those advocating a competences-based approach to professional learning and those supporting the notion of the reflective practitioner. This argument is about the nature of professionalism and a continuation of the debate about the practicality and desirability of defining performance in the professional field. A 'behaviourist' approach to the improvement of professional practice is regarded as inadequate by many people because its formulaic character over-rides the key ability of the professional to be appropriately responsive to circumstances. The debate therefore also centres on the mechanisms of personal change and whether a simple focus on knowledge and skills is adequate to bring about behavioural change. Reflective practice, with its testing of beliefs and assumption, places far more emphasis on cognitive processes, internal factors and personal growth within the job than the more straightforward process of 'gap filling' implied by a techno-rational approach to development where one identifies a missing skill or area of knowledge and undertakes an appropriate course to 'fill it in'.

In this book we shall argue that a key aspect of improving performance is the nature of the learning that must underpin any change process and that changing practice within a professional context is not simply substituting one set of routine actions for another set. Given our belief in the need to improve effectiveness it follows that models of learning that can support the improvement of performance need to be explored. This may involve opportunities for 'new' learning or opportunities to review and reorganise prior learning which, in turn may, lead to 'new' learning. A critical outcome is the facility to reshape or reconstruct practices by constructing knowledge about and through action.

Eraut (1994), in critiquing the common distinction between knowledge, skills and attitudes in discussion of teacher development, argues that, in this formulation, knowledge is limited to 'propositional' knowledge that does not include any suggestion of performance: it is 'knowing that'. However, for successful performance another form of knowledge is critical, what he calls 'process knowledge' (which can incorporate propositional knowledge): 'as knowing how to conduct the various processes that contribute to professional action' (*ibid.*: 107).

Increasingly, the literature on the continuing development of teachers and school managers acknowledges the importance of 'process knowledge'. A variety of terms are used to describe this. Hagger (1997), discussing initial teacher education, refers to it as teachers' 'craft knowledge' and is concerned with student teachers being able to access the craft knowledge of experienced teachers within the classroom. This view of knowledge is now regarded as underpinning the development of experienced teachers and managers. The acquisition of this process knowledge is dependent upon the formation and testing of ideas in action by the practitioner (Bourner *et al.*, 2000: 25).

In this sense professional development has at its heart a willed personal/professional 'transformation' that implies that issues of motivation and self-perception are critical. Part of developing process knowledge will be the development of ideas and beliefs about education; equally important are ideas about the self as a practitioner/professional. Often specific approaches and practices used by teachers in classrooms are based on their beliefs about education and what kind of teacher they are. These beliefs may relate to a broad area such as relationships with pupils, for example ('I am the type of teacher who is friendly and positive with the children because I think they need to feel secure to learn') or to a specific pedagogic practice ('I like to concentrate on the teaching of spelling because I am the kind of teacher who believes in giving the children a good grounding in the basics').

In reforming practice, an important dimension is the potential change or modification of the self-concept as part of the learning process. Fundamental improvement of performance has to be explored in terms of a learning process in which both cognitive and emotional processes come into play as practitioners rethink their own role within an organisation and within the wider environment. Nixon *et al.* (1996) argue for a recovery of the Aristotelian conception of what it is to develop as a person over the whole of one's life. This argument places personal growth within the social domain where we have a mutual responsibility towards each other: 'To learn, then, is to develop understanding which leads into, and grows out of action; to discover a sense of agency that enables us, not only to define and make ourselves, but to do so actively participating in the creation of a world in which, inescapably, we live together' (*ibid.*: 50).

In professions such as medicine, social work and teaching, the process of interaction with a fellow human being or group of fellow human beings is the core of the practice of that professional. However, we need to move further than that and to recognise that Eraut's (1994: 236) fourth area of accountability ('an obligation that is professional as well as contractual to contribute to the quality of one's organisation') is essentially about growth within a social setting. This approach highlights both the significance of the social domain as a place of learning and the importance of the workplace as a learning context. As Nixon *et al.* (1996: 51) propose: 'it is not just that any competence is learnt with and through others, but that the subjectivities which define what we become as persons, and therefore our agency, are social creations.' Our concerns with the dynamics of organisational learning, personal learning and improved performance will be evident in subsequent chapters.

Having set out some of the parameters for the book in this introduction, the rest of the text is divided into three broad sections. The
first of these looks at the development of the policy agenda for performance management in the schools sector and it gives an overview
of current developments in the field. The second explores some of the
more theoretical issues involved in improving professional practice
and different approaches to work-based learning. The third looks at
the practical consequences of introducing a mixed approach to
improving performance and some of the lessons that emerged for
schools, individuals and those supporting them in implementing the
Scottish Qualification for Headship programme.

2

The concern with performance and continuing professional development

As a starting point for this chapter, two questions need to be addressed: first, why is there such an emphasis on performance management in policy terms? And, secondly, within this policy framework, what does 'performance management' mean for schools and teachers and, more recently, for local government? It could be argued that the improvement of performance (the key dimension of performance management) has been mislaid in the effort expended over the years in creating an elaborate regulatory system that demands easily quantifiable levels of performance. For over quarter of a century in the UK performance management has been vested in a variety of initiatives, while the central theme of improving performance has become submerged in the debates and 'angst' associated with the systems introduced to monitor and evaluate school and teacher effectiveness.

Initiatives associated with this concern for performance have been supported by staff development (for example, training for appraisal). Staff development is regarded as a key strategy to bring about change in practice in schools. However, the concern for performance and the current development of ideas about the nature of performance call for a discussion about the significance of continuing professional development. Over the last four years in England and Wales there has been a raft of continuing professional development (CPD) strategies and initiatives, launched through a range of green paper consultations and legislation. Scotland has had its own inquiry (the McCrone Committee) and subsequently the Chartered Teacher Scotland initiative. We will set out the changing policy context and trace the emergence of the identified 'need' for teachers' continuing professional learning or CPD to be part of the framework for the management of the performance. Key areas we will pursue include: the concepts concerning how teachers learn that underpinned the various CPD initiatives; the dominance of a content-led CPD agenda; and the recent moves to work-based learning both north and south of the border with the resulting more action-orientated approach.

Establishing the performance management agenda

The two significant and intertwined external influences on developments in the schools sector over the last 25 years are, first, those that have been policy directed (often ideologically driven and based on a set of beliefs about how the state ought to operate in relation to the delivery of public services) and, secondly, social change that has impacted directly on schools or led to policy responses.

Three discernible stages are identifiable in the development of the performance management agenda in schools:

1) An initial emphasis on organisational effectiveness at school level.
2) Subsequently, increasing concerns with measures to improve the performance of individuals, both school managers and teachers.
3) Concerns with measures to improve the performance of school systems as local authorities have come under scrutiny.

The debate initiated by Callaghan's Ruskin College speech in 1976 signalled a concern about standards in education and the need to make schools and teachers more accountable. The ideas developed by Keith Joseph and the New Right that were put into practice during the 'Thatcher era' post-1979 were seminal (for example, developments such as enhanced governing bodies, the local management of schools, a National Curriculum, establishing standards or competences for teachers and introducing regular and rigorous inspections). Such implementation has nevertheless continued in similar vein under New Labour (Ball, 1999) using both statutory and economic means to ensure compliance. At the same time, a broad set of social changes had (and are having) direct effects on the provision of schooling. Such influences include:

- Changes in the labour market and the structure of work.
- Technological innovation.
- The changing role of women.
- Structural changes in the nature of the family.
- A growing polarisation between rich and poor (child poverty).
- An increasing cultural diversity.
- Globalisation.
- Ecological changes.

The new public management

Since the early 1980s the functions of the state in the West have been restructured in the face of new political orthodoxy requiring public services to become efficient and effective by adopting the practices and approaches used in the private sector. Citizens were to become customers, and a new consumerist, market-driven democracy based on the notion of 'stakeholding' was to replace the postwar social democratic consensus on the rights of all citizens to universal services free at the point of delivery (Clarke and Newman, 1997). The terms 'managerialism' or new public management (Walsh, 1995) were used to describe the resulting wholesale importation of practices from the private sector into the running of state agencies and services (such as public health, social services and education) in order to introduce 'market forces' and sound commercial practices.

The major challenge was to alter the prevailing bureaucratic culture of the public services. Stress was laid on abandoning traditional administrative relationships structured as professional bureaucracies by: 'combining culture management (the creation of meanings and purposes) with performance management (measuring what really matters). The aim was to create the transparent organisation where everyone is responsible for achieving corporate objectives and everyone is enterprising in pursuit of them' (Clarke and Newman, 1997: 62). There was an emphasis on strengthening line management and 'the right to manage'. Decisions were not to be left to the professionals, who were seen as more concerned with preserving their own interests than in serving the needs of their clients. These principles, embodied in the Citizen's Charter (1991), were seen as an important tool in bringing about the required change in attitudes and relationships.

The two prime means of breaking down the public service bureaucracies were the fragmentation of large organisations into smaller units and the marketisation of relationships through the creation of a division between purchasers and providers. In this new model of delivery there are essentially three elements:

1) A central core responsible for strategy and policy-making.
2) Purchasing bodies responsible for setting and monitoring standards of delivery.
3) Service providers.

In many cases service provision has been contracted out to the private sector and there is a continuing thrust, through such policies as Best Value (DETR, 1997), to promote this trend, which is now beginning to extend into public education (for example, in the plans for the management of Education Action Zones (DfEE, 1997) and for public/private funding initiatives). Additionally, the use of development/business planning, with a focus on action, began to permeate many public sector organisations and services. Whether or not the resulting services have been improved is debatable but, certainly, where they have been retained they have functioned under conditions where resourcing has been significantly reduced.

Managing performance in the schools sector

Schools were subject to the same forces. They were faced with a decline in absolute funding and an increased demand for performance. This arose because schools were now confronted by a widening client group occasioned by the growth in youth unemployment, which led to a rapid extension of schooling for the majority of youngsters as well as improving standards of attainment necessitated by the decline in manufacturing and heavy industry and the associated loss of jobs that were physically rather than intellectually challenging. Increasingly a highly skilled and well educated workforce was seen as a necessity to work in the new industries associated with computerisation and advanced technology.

The educational establishment was regarded as the main barrier to school improvement. One way of breaking up this establishment was by devolving responsibility to school level through decentralisation of resources and through granting schools increased autonomy to determine the implementation of policy at site level. School effectiveness research provided a useful justification for restructuring. A number of influential research studies into the effectiveness of schools in both the USA (Summers and Wolfe, 1977; Brookover *et al.*, 1978; Goodlad, 1979) and Britain (Rutter *et al.*, 1979; Mortimore *et al.*, 1988) demonstrated that schools had a differential and measurable effect on the attainment outcomes of their pupils. Such research identified a number of features associated with school effectiveness and these, suitably combined with managerial orthodoxies, began to form a basis for policy development.

Caldwell and Spinks (1988: 7) crystallise the argument in *The Self-Managing School*:

> They [Peters and Waterman, 1982] found that excellent companies are both centralised and decentralised, pushing autonomy down to the shop floor or production team for some functions but being 'fanatical centralists about the core values they hold dear'. The parallel in

education is the centralised determination of broad goals and purposes of education accompanied by decentralised decision-making about the means by which these goals and purposes will be achieved, with those people who are decentralised being accountable to those centralised for the achievement of outcomes.

In 1982, the Centre for Educational Research and Innovation (CERI) of the Organisation for Economic Co-operation and Development (OECD) set up the International School Improvement Project (ISIP) to investigate the use of institutional planning techniques at individual-school level (Hopkins, 1987). The association between this and the changing attitude towards public services was clear in the words of the director: 'Strengthening the school's capacity to deal with change, for example, reflects assuming an increased responsibility for its own development' (Van Velzen, 1985: 11). This resonated with the notion that teachers and schools take direct responsibility for the quality of the service they offered to the parents and children in their local community and it was their responsibility to deal directly with the outcomes of lack of investment in the service (Gewirtz *et al.*, 1995).

In the late 1980s, the OECD promoted work on international educational performance indicators, building on work done to develop quality standards initially applied to commercial organisations such as ISO 9000. By the early 1990s the approaches advocated for school improvement began increasingly to reflect the teachings of total quality management. The term 'quality' became a dominant and constant feature in much of the literature aimed at school managers (Bayne-Jardine and Holly, 1994; Hopkins *et al.*, 1996).

Developments in the UK

Against this backdrop of the findings of international studies on school effectiveness and improvement, the UK government effectively established a triad of devices to bring about school improvement:

1) Development planning.
2) School inspection.
3) Parental choice informed by publication of results.

However, as education systems within the UK became more focused on the question of school effectiveness and improvement, there were however different responses in different parts of the country.

England and Wales

As part of the drive towards market accountability, the Education Act 1986 gave parents and the local community – via an empowered governing body – greater control over their schools. In line with managerialist doctrine, the Education Reform Act (ERA) 1988 also introduced a National Curriculum for primary and secondary schools, thus providing a centralised control of the curriculum and assessment that effectively bypassed the traditional responsibilities of teachers and local authorities. Schools could also be made more accountable through new assessment processes that would enable the government to use and publish comparative data on attainment so parents could make choices between schools on the basis of their performance.

The position of LEAs was altered with the introduction of grant-maintained status for schools where parents could elect to take the school out of LEA control. A further blow to the LEAs came with the introduction of the local management of schools on a statutory basis under the ERA. This was predicated on the notion the unit of resource would be individual pupils, thus effectively equalising the basis for the funding of schools regardless of their context.

By 1992 school development plans became the official vehicle for inspection in England and Wales (OfSTED, 1993). The structure for school inspection had been completely overhauled and a regime of regular four-yearly school inspections was introduced along with the publication of inspection reports to parents and the general public.

Recent years have seen the role of the LEA in England change to give a greater emphasis on monitoring for school improvement, rather than supporting, mentoring and developing teachers and headteachers – and this is now true in Scotland as well but approaches to intervention differ. LEAs (through the DfEE code of practice) are required to intervene in schools in inverse proportion to success, further fostering the notion of the autonomy of the effective schools and placing the responsibility for raising standards of attainment and achievement clearly on the shoulders of headteachers, governors and teachers. In England, LEAs have effectively been reduced to acting as local agencies of the government following central directives. In this regard the Act represents the final move away from the principles of social democracy that informed the Education Act 1944 (Hannon, 1999). The establishment of statutory Education Action Zones and Excellence in Cities partnerships follows this theme, with schools agreeing to raise their targets in return for substantial sums of curriculum and staff development funding. The growth of school self-evaluation, using OfSTED criteria, and the birth of performance management linked to pupil achievement, partially completes this fix on the schools standards agenda.

The Scottish experience

Scottish developments broadly followed the direction of those in England and Wales. However, while the pacing and extent of the reforms was different, very similar areas were targeted. The variations included the following:

- A greater emphasis on school self-evaluation, although a more frequent inspection regime was also introduced.
- Greater autonomy for LEAs in proposing and implementing schemes for devolved school management.
- A change in school governance through the introduction of school boards, although the power of the boards was very limited when compared to governing bodies south of the border.

While no formal national curriculum exists in Scotland, the *5–14 Guidelines* (SOED, 1994b), were used to introduce a new form of national testing as the basis for providing comparative data on the functioning of primary schools. Testing was defeated by the united resistance of parents' and teachers' groups. Only now are performance data on primary schools coming into the public domain as part of the target-setting initiative introduced in 1998.

Education is a devolved responsibility of the new Scottish Parliament, and MSPs have been keen to confirm the distinctiveness of Scottish education. Policy divergence is already evident (for example, student fees in higher education). More schools with distinctive approaches may now emerge and this may again encourage parents to choose particular experiences for their children where they are available. Implicit in these developments seems to be a change in the notion of performance, allowing for greater local diversity.

The pressure for improvement is now being applied beyond the school. For example, the role of local government in the education system is increasingly being scrutinised in terms of performance. Familiar mechanisms are being extended. HMI inspections of LEAs are mandated by the first Education Act of the Scottish Parliament (Scottish Executive, 2000), with the statutory requirement that LEAs produce annual improvement plans containing agreed and explicit performance targets for their schools. This will close the final gap in the performance management system that will in future encompass individuals, schools and school systems.

The performance of teachers and school managers

More recently the policy agenda has increasingly centred on measures to improve the performance of individuals, both school managers and teachers. This interest in individual performance has gone through a number of repetitive stages because of failures of implementation, especially with respect to the appraisal of teachers.

In 1984, Sir Keith Joseph, the Conservative Secretary of State for Education, suggested the 'weeding out' of incompetent teachers and was the first minister to link teacher appraisal with accountability and pay. Goddard and Emerson (1997) identify two distinct approaches to the early initiatives in appraisal:

1) *The professional development approach* concerned with teacher career plans, affirming what teachers do well and offering opportunities for further development.
2) *The accountability approach* that seeks to identify weaknesses in performance and to produce evidence about incompetent teachers.

Surveys in the mid-1990s, such as Wragg and Conrad (1996), demonstrated a mixed reaction to appraisal, with teachers acting favourably where the process had been handled skilfully and sensitively. However, some teachers were hostile and were supported in this by their unions.

The shortcomings of appraisal identified in the MORI survey into CPD in 1995 prompted the Secretary of State to ask the Teacher Training Agency (TTA) and OfSTED to undertake a review that showed variable practices across the country and the need to improve the observation, feedback and target-setting skills of the profession. The green paper (DfEE, 1998) and the introduction of the performance management process have taken five more years to move to addressing these deficits.

The TTA's early work fed into the publication in 1998 of the green paper *Teachers: Meeting the Challenge of Change.* This set out the government's agenda for modernising the teaching profession through promoting excellent school leadership, through recruiting and retaining high-quality classroom teachers and through providing better support for all teachers. This was followed by a consultation document on pay and performance that sought views on the proposals and vision in the green paper. It was confirmed that the government's vision of a modernised teaching profession is attached substantially to the concept of performance management now embodied in the performance management framework (DfEE, 2000a) and regulations for headteacher and teacher performance review documents. The espoused theory is that 'good, well-motivated headteachers and teachers are the key to success in every school', and the underlying belief is that by making 'a substantial investment in the pay, professional development, support and working conditions of teachers' the government can 'expect in return, a universal commitment to achieving high standards'.

The DfEE states that the regulations for headteacher and teacher performance review will build on existing good practice in teacher appraisal. Clearly those schools that have invested in the development of appraisal skills and processes over the past decade, perhaps through an Investors in People policy, will be able to draw on their prior practice in the implementation of the performance management policy. This new policy affirms the centrality of the relationship between the professional performance of the school, through its school development plan, and the professional performance of its staff. It is evidenced through individual objectives and action plans that in turn are firmly located in the school development plan and its targets to raise standards of pupil performance. This view of a rational synergy of review and action planning for improvement at all levels of the school community appears to establish, for the first time, the entitlement of teachers and headteachers to receive well planned and high-quality professional development in response to their identified needs. The associated shift to school-based assessment of colleagues' competency this initiative holds (for example, in relation to the threshold standard and to performance related pay) presents a major challenge for middle managers and team leaders in particular.

Many writers have claimed that the introduction of performance management, evidenced first of all through the troubled threshold payment system, is in effect the introduction of performance-related pay (PRP), with its underlying belief that if workers' wages are geared explicitly to their output they perform more efficiently. The problem with such a concept is that the output of schoolteachers (and headteachers) is the education of their pupils, which is multidimensional and not easy to measure. Teaching is based on teamwork and co-operative effort and, hence, rewarding one teacher and not another is difficult; individual PRP, it is argued, reduces co-operation between teachers. Assessment, even by colleagues using peer review, may promote a divisive and threatening culture, and pupils' individual performances and value-added achievements are difficult to measure accurately.

This turbulent story of managing cultural change and the modernisation of the teaching profession through the reform of teachers' pay involved a High Court judgment in 2000, which found against the DfEE in relation to its threshold pay processes. However this was a minor barrier, quietly overcome, and the threshold payments of £2,000 are securely in the pockets of eligible teachers. With threshold payments accepted and the setting of objectives through annual appraisal underway, it can be argued the government's performance management and rewards policy is now being implemented and it will be interesting to see if it is successful.

Appraisal was introduced into Scotland in 1991 with the emphasis on professional development. The reaction was comparable with the English experience: implementation was haphazard and largely unsuccessful because both teachers and employers regarded the entire venture with considerable suspicion, and teacher resistance proved effective.

A re-launch of the 'appraisal' process was also attempted in Scotland with the reintroduction of staff review and development (SOEID, 1998b), which led to further limited adoption. The pay and conditions of service agreement (SEED, 2001) with the Scottish teaching profession, following the McCrone Inquiry, has avoided PRP and notions of threshold payments. Rather an enhanced pay scale for teachers willing to undertake professional development leading to Chartered Teacher status over a period of years is to be introduced. A linking of proof of successful performance to pay has been 'rejected' in Scotland, although the terms for recognition as a Chartered Teacher do make a direct link between the acquisition of accredited CPD and levels of pay.

How has provision for the professional development of serving teachers reflected and developed in line with performance management initiatives?

From INSET to CPD

The growth of provision and the control of the curriculum

In 1972, the James Report (DES, 1972) recommended a large expansion of in-service education and training (INSET). The committee argued that effective and successful teachers who enjoy a high degree of work satisfaction tended to be those who had the benefit of in-service opportunities. They argued that in-service training or professional development would be 'the quickest, most effective and most economical way of improving the quality of education in schools and colleges, and of raising the standards, morale and status of the teaching profession' (*ibid*.: 72). These arguments assumed that the association between the two variables of engagement in CPD and effective practice was causal and did not signal any debate as to why and how in-service improved performance.

The post-James period in England was dominated by ten years of expansion of training programmes 'in a somewhat haphazard way and in an uneven fashion' (Buckley, 1985: 86). Nevertheless there was a discernible movement towards a more school-focused approach fuelled by early experiments with school improvement strategies, such as the Guidelines for Review and Internal Development (GRIDS) initiative sponsored by the Schools' Council Development Committee (McMahon *et al.*, 1984) and the development of interest and involvement in teacher action research and curriculum development inspired by Stenhouse (1975). Both approaches supported early attempts to structure and underpin work-based learning.

In the mid-1970s we can see alternative models of CPD operating, the first of which focused on how practice collectively can be enhanced and the second of which was concerned with ensuring the relevance of the content of courses to practice. Initiatives such as GRIDS and ideas of collaborative action research did put forward a more rounded understanding of teacher learning, with an emphasis on experimenting with and reviewing specific aspects of practice collectively. However, despite interest, these models were not pursued in subsequent decades to any great degree. During this period CPD was the major mechanism through which changes to the curriculum and changes to the management of schools could be implemented. The concern was to ensure that the content of courses would promote effective implementation of specific curricular or management initiatives.

The white paper *Better Schools* (DES, 1985) resulted in a series of criticisms about the effectiveness of in-service delivered by LEAs and increasing dissatisfaction with provision was evident. Circular 6/86 (DES, 1986) established a system of ring fencing money so that the content and focus of in-service was increasingly under government control. At the same time a more marketised approach to CPD provision was encouraged through the development of purchaser/provider relationships designed to help unlock the pernicious hold of the educational establishment on teacher development (Glover and Law, 1996).

The education standards agenda was typified by the increasing involvement of central government in the curriculum and the introduction of the National Curriculum with its associated assessment requirements from 1989 onwards. As a result, in the years following the ERA, in-service was dominated by the introduction and implementation of the National Curriculum and the local management of schools initiative.

Any debate about the nature and outcomes of CPD was substantially set back as the implementation of the central government agenda steam-rollered any earlier engagement in organisational development and developing ideas of reflexive practice. School development planning during the 1990s was dominated by the need to operationalise the National Curriculum agenda, inhibiting its use as a vehicle for self-evaluation and improvement, and in-service provision was dominated by courses designed to tell them 'how to do it'. This burst of centrally defined activity did not substantially change approaches to promoting professional development although it did entail the introduction of INSET days that promoted the development of whole-school provision whereby all the teachers in a school shared the same learning experience. Opportunities for the discussion and exchange of classroom experience were substantially increased.

Dominance of provision by nationally defined curricula has thus legitimated the increase in centrally prescribed professional development which, in the last five years, has resulted in a major target on the national literacy and numeracy strategies for primary-aged pupils and the Key Stage 3 strategy, focused mainly on English, maths and science. These strategies mark a further development in this centrally directed trend in that they specify not only what is to be taught and assessed but also the teaching methods to be adopted.

In 1997, the DfEE established the Standards and Effectiveness Unit, and there appears to be evidence that policy under this unit is now shifting from a heavy emphasis on accountability, ambitious standards and intervention to access to professional development, best practice, clear targets and devolved responsibility. What is significant here is the conceptualisation of the process of CPD. In these developments we again see an emphasis on the content of provision as a means of bringing about change. Courses and other development opportunities through the EIC and EAZ initiatives tend to focus on what is to be delivered in the classroom.

Barber and Phillips (2000) have spoken recently of the inter-relationship between beliefs (values) and behaviours in terms of the process of change; they appear to support strongly the notion that 'behaviours shape beliefs'. They view the practice of changed behaviours as of central importance in the design of provision for professional learning. Their explanation for the success of the basic skills intervention would seem to be that teachers' experiences of putting into place the learned behaviours of teaching the literacy hour have led to the development of desirable 'beliefs', 'values' and 'consciousness' – presumably about what constitutes a high standard of teaching in literacy.

The second major strand of provision, which traces its origins to the mid-1980s, is that of management development. Initially this was heavily targeted at headteachers in order to equip them to take on their new managerial duties under the terms of local management of schools in England and Wales. The emphasis again has been on 'how to do it' rather than any examination of values, beliefs and purposes (Duignan and MacPherson, 1992; Grace, 1995). The pattern of provision has been for the maintenance of national control over provision for headteachers whilst provision for middle managers has been left as a local responsibility. However this position is being tightened up in the south by the formation of the National College for School Leadership (NCSL), which is likely to exercise purchaser quality control over provision for both heads and middle managers. It can be argued that the challenge for the new NCSL over the next year or so will be to develop and support school leaders to manage threatening cultural change expertly in relation to performance management in the midst of major teacher recruitment, retention and morale issues.

Standards and work-based learning

Since teaching became an all-graduate profession in the early 1980s, the use of competences and national standards to determine the design of the course of study and the award of Qualified Teacher Status (QTS) have become increasingly central to initial teacher education (ITE) to the point where there is now a prescribed common curriculum in England and Wales. The significance of such standards is that they switch the emphasis from the content of the curriculum for teacher education to the outcomes of the process and are meant to underline the primary value of the *practice* of teaching as opposed to the theoretical leanings of the educational establishment embodied in the teacher education institutes (TEIs).

Responsibility for the initial training and assessment of teachers is now equally shared and often led by schools in partnership with higher education institutes (HEIs). The past decade has seen a major shift in the coaching of ITE students by their school-based mentors. This is no longer the domain of the HEI tutor who, instead, has a quality assurance role in a fully worked-through ITE work-based learning system. The introduction of the Licensed and Graduate (or

Registered) Teacher Training Schemes from the early 1990s onwards placed an added responsibility for work-based learning and assessment on a set of national standards for teachers and managers in schools. The impending birth of the Fast Track scheme of training will place yet another one.

Within these mentoring developments there are some suggestions about the nature and process of teacher development that could be built upon in developing a school-focused CPD founded on a coherent work-based model of teacher learning. The public description of the tasks of a teacher has proved useful as a basis for designing opportunities for the development of practice in schools and for assessing performance. Additionally, there can be no doubt that those teachers and headteachers in England and Wales who have engaged in the role of mentor to initial and newly qualified teachers over the past decade have also had to develop their work-based learning skills and appropriate processes in school to support this. In the pursuit of improving standards of teaching and learning these involve the higher-order skills and qualities of collaborative planning, listening, demonstrating, facilitating, observing, assessing, collaborative teaching, discussing and supporting self-evaluation. As such, mentoring development can make a major contribution to the development of schools as 'learning organisations' or, as Pedlar and his co-researchers term it, a 'learning company' that 'facilitates the learning of all its members and which continuously transforms itself' (Pedlar, 1991, in Stewart and McGoldrick, 1996).

The notion of a mentoring organisation, if only during the initial and first year of teaching, is therefore significant to the discussion of performance management and work-based learning in England and Wales. A school that is a 'mentoring organisation' provides a model of a social system that exists to serve common interests (that is, high standards of teaching and learning) through co-operative efforts. The value of this is being supported by the practice of a number of HEIs that recognise their training schools through accreditation. The TTA/DfEE now has a system of allocating 'Training School' status to schools, and there are also Beacon Schools where strengths in mentoring and professional development are recognised and rewarded by the DfEE.

However, alongside mentoring it is the potential of national standards or competences of teachers that has been taken up strongly in the area of CPD for serving teachers in recent years. The development of teaching standards in England and Wales was moved forward apace by the TTA, established by Act of Parliament in September 1994 with the statutory objective of contributing to raising standards of teaching. At first it concerned itself with initial teacher training but in March 1995 the Secretary of State discussed with the TTA its involvement in the development of more targeted and effective continuing professional development. This involvement resulted in an infamous MORI survey of the nature and cost of existing CPD provision, which resulted in the overall judgement that: 'CPD currently taking place in most schools appears to operate on an *ad hoc* basis with no real linkage across schools' development planning, personal development planning and teachers' appraisals' (*ibid.: 27*).

The TTA were also empowered to consider strategic approaches to managing and focusing CPD. Their consultation identified weaknesses and variation in CPD, particularly in relation to meeting identified needs, inadequate planning, evaluation and follow-up to ensure a direct impact on teaching and learning. The more recent inspection of TTA-funded INSET in HEIs has also used these criteria to assess the quality of the provision and to grade it accordingly. Further, OfSTED is being directed by the DfEE through its school inspections to focus on the assessment of school management of CPD and performance management systems. This more recent data will provide valuable comparisons with the TTA surveys of the mid-1990s, which tended to give a 'poor' impression of teachers' professional learning, whether school or LEA/HEI based. The TTA concluded that, in a modernised profession, teachers should take responsibility for developing their own knowledge, understanding and skills – there were no statements concerning entitlement or funding beyond induction (see Table 2.1).

Table 2.1   National CPD priorities in England and Wales in 1995

- Leadership and management of schools.
- Heads of department in secondary schools.
- Subject co-ordinators in primary phase.
- Subject knowledge of Key Stage 2 teachers.
- Effective teaching in 14–19 phase.
- The use of IT to improve pupils' achievements.
- Effective teaching for early years children.
- Special education needs co-ordinators.

The TTA's advice concluded with one major and pervasive proposal. This was the setting of national standards of excellence for teachers in key roles in order to provide a more coherent approach to improving teaching quality. They proposed the key roles of:

- newly qualified teachers;
- expert teachers;
- experts in subject leadership and management; and
- experts in school leadership and management.

National standards have been in active use since 1996, especially in relation to newly qualified teachers (NQTs) and aspiring headteachers, through the NQT scheme and, latterly, through the Leadership Programme for Serving Headteachers (LPSH).

Qualifications for headship

The first use of standards in post-initial teacher education was in the professional development of aspiring headteachers. The Major government committed itself to the development of a qualification for headteachers that would become mandatory for anyone applying for the post of headteacher – a policy that was continued under the Labour government.

The National Professional Qualification for Headship (NPQH), introduced in 1994, has had a chequered history in terms of the relevance of the assessment regime and the quality of the training provision through 'private' consortia. It was suspended in 1998 and subsequently relaunched in 2000 in a form that laid much greater stress on work-based learning.

The other relevant developments are the implementation of the Threshold and Advanced Teacher Standards neither of which have been linked to programmes of professional development but both of which have involved the preparation and submission of portfolios of evidence derived from practice in school and in that rather loose sense that work-based learning is being validated through the assessment process.

The Scottish experience and CPD response

The Scottish experience of INSET closely resembles the approaches discussed above. A series of reports emanating from the National Committee on the In-service Training of Teachers (NCITT, 1979; 1984a; 1984b) suggested an emerging INSET-command economy. Certainly a tradition of greater central development of the curriculum and national co-ordination of INSET priorities and format dominated official thinking, but Scotland's relative size and population do provide a manageable context for national provision. From the late 1980s, CPD was geared to major National Curriculum initiatives such as the 5–14 Development Programme and Higher Still (Roger and Hartley, 1990), which specified not only what was to be taught and assessed but also the teaching methods to be adopted; the management training that should be designed to support the implementation of devolved management of schools; development planning; and the appraisal of teachers (O'Brien, 1995). The approach has received mixed reviews. For example, national training for appraisal was very well received but criticisms of the quality of some of the national CPD provision associated with Higher Still (SOED, 1994a) have been vociferous. INSET was 'marketised' in 1994 when the TEIs lost their dedicated staffing and when new trading relationships between provider and purchaser emerged.

In Scotland, competences have been in use in ITE programmes since 1992. However, Scotland abandoned experimentation in mentoring in the face of strong professional resistance. While partnership between schools and HEIs has been strengthened it remains problematic and often misunderstood, and there are developing proposals for formal partnership contracts. The GTC (Scotland) has long played a key role in ensuring competence in professional training through its course accreditation processes in ITE, and there were efforts to develop probationer support programmes (including the use of the competences as the basis for planning development) during this period. However, no uniformly successful provision exists for new recruits (Draper *et al.*, 1993).

In his report on teacher education and training, Sutherland (1997) concluded that greater coherence was required in the arrangements for CPD. He argued for an encompassing national framework to include probation and induction and the range, types and levels of CPD undertaken by teachers. The response was a consultation document: *Proposals for developing a framework for continuing professional development for the teaching profession in Scotland* (SOEID, 1998b). A framework for CPD that might contain 'guidance for teachers, schools, and education authorities on the competences, standards and qualifications required in the wide range of teaching and management roles that teachers undertake at different stages in their careers' was proposed. This would include the development of statements of competences or standards and a structure of qualifications and awards that would give recognition to teachers' increased remits and professional skills.

The outcomes of the consultation exercise on a framework for CPD (SOEID, 1998b) endorsed Sutherland's (1997) belief that such a framework would help to raise the standards of teaching and, consequently, levels of attainment by pupils. It would also help LAs and schools in taking decisions on the allocation of resources for development and training, and it would help provide more information on development activities and qualifications. Work has begun on addressing a number of aspects, including the Chartered Teacher (CT) initiative. Currently the details of this initiative are being developed through a consortium comprising Arthur Andersen plc and the universities of Edinburgh and Strathclyde, who are conducting a further consultation in order to develop an appropriate standard and to pilot CPD for CT status (Chartered Teacher Partnership, 2001). Evident within the initial consultation document is a view that CPD provision should be largely classroom related to enhance practice, though the problematic issue of a generalist focus on teaching and learning versus the development of specialisms is raised as a key question. The quality of the provision is also a concern, with various means of ensuring a standard through accreditation as a professional and/or academic award being proposed. The question of how teachers learn is dealt with only implicitly, with suggestions for a combination of academic study and work-based learning: 'The focus of the Standard for Chartered Teacher programme should be on improvement of professional understanding and action; and both academic study and work-based learning would be seen as essential components of this development' (*ibid.*, 2001: 8).

Although the importance of the school as the site for work-based learning is evident here, this model seems to focus on teacher development as an individual enterprise. Although the enhancement of practice is an underpinning principle established in this initiative, the context of the school as the site for learning is not examined in any detail. The status of CT obviously has to be an individual award but the learning programme to be pursued seems to focus on the individual teacher rather than collaborative effort with teachers within a school working together to build an improving school rather than focusing on the isolated practice of individual teachers.

Completing the modernisation project

So, 30 years or so after the James Committee, its advice might appear to be heeded with a recent £90 million investment in a CPD strategy and the hundreds of millions spent on targeted literacy and numeracy training and materials for Key Stages 1, 2 and 3 in England and Wales. Supporters of the English literacy and numeracy strategies have already pointed to evidence of its early success in raising standards at primary level after just two years of implementation.

CPD is regarded as pivotal in the improvement of performance, and there is currently a vast array of initiatives. What we see in these developments again is a number of different elements that could contribute to a more coherent conceptualisation of the nature of teacher development and its contribution to improving performance in schools.

Prior to the UK general election of 2001, the Labour government produced a new green paper, *Schools: Building on Success* (DfEE, 2001c), taking forward the 1997 white paper *Excellence in Schools*, which set the vision for much of the educational reform discussed above. Besides the 'diversity' agenda, this green paper includes a strong commitment to systematic professional development in England and Wales, including:

- extending the provision of Best Practice Research Scholarships;
- offering sabbaticals and international professional development opportunities to teachers;
- extending professional bursaries for teacher professional development; and
- increasing the provision of early professional development in the second and third years of teaching.

This marks the revival of one of the earlier approaches to teacher development – that of the teacher as researcher – which is linked in policy terms with the notion of 'finding out what works': a phrase that usefully glides over a number of ontological and practical issues. This notion of the teacher researcher has been a popular strand in government policy since Hargreaves' (1996) condemnation of formal education research and the call for a more practical approach based on practitioner involvement, which has been linked through to earlier ideas about raising student achievement through practice-focused staff development (Joyce *et al.*,1999).

The Introduction to the CPD strategy document (DfEE, 2001b) states it is designed to modernise and raise standards in the profession and will only work 'if teachers' confidence and competence are nurtured and supported through investment in CPD, so that high performance and improved opportunity go hand in hand' (*ibid.*).

To achieve this end, the policy document creates a code of practice ('Good Value CPD'), establishing the principles of high-quality CPD for providers and consumers and promoting the use of the Investors in People standard in schools presently adopted by 50 per cent of schools in England. It envisages the strategic use of a CPD website and the expansion of Beacon, Specialist and Training Schools and Advanced Skills Teachers to disseminate and promote the use of good practice in CPD through the development of local and regional networks supported by LEAs and HEIs working in partnership with schools. The strategy also contains a commitment to completing a review of the National Professional Standards Framework for teachers at key points in their career: end of induction; middle management/team leader; threshold; Advanced Skills Teacher; special educational needs co-ordinator; and headteacher. It also provides guidance on creating a professional development portfolio and on building on the use of the Career Entry Profiles and NQT and NPQH portfolios now in use.

The rationale underpinning the national CPD strategy and the school-based nature of most of the initiatives it promotes is worthy of further discussion here, since work-based learning to improve performance is clearly at the heart of the strategy. The DfEE (2001b: 3) states it wants to encourage high-quality professional development because:

> ... we know from talking to schools that a commitment to the development of every member of staff – teachers and support staff – frequently leads to the creation of an open, supportive and collaborative culture across the school; greater self esteem, self confidence and enthusiasm; better quality teaching; a real desire amongst staff to continue learning; and greater capacity in the school as a whole for continuous self improvement'.

This reference to the collaborative culture of a 'learning organisation' supports the notion discussed earlier in this chapter of the importance of building on the successes of those schools that have promoted a culture of learning, often through a mentoring approach that results in the formation of a self-critical community of practitioners, which has been well documented by earlier researchers such as Carr and Kemmis (1990) and Lomax (1990). Does the DfEE CPD strategy, therefore, reflect a move away from the large-scale, somewhat behaviourist approach to professional learning to be seen in the National Literacy Strategy and National Numeracy Strategy initiatives towards a more cognitive and diverse set of opportunities for teachers and managers to engage in research and reflection on practice?

Certainly, the emphasis the strategy holds for individual teacher empowerment and ownership of their professional learning is potentially significant. Much will depend on school budgets and management systems, of course, but the message supports the idea of teachers identifying their own professional learning needs and, through applications for research grants, professional bursaries, international visits or standards funds to action plan their own response to that need. This ownership by the profession of their own professional learning is enshrined in a range of statutory instruments since, as the DfEE state, 'taking responsibility for one's own professional development is increasingly a requirement in other professions'. The School Teachers Review Body (STRB) has agreed to an updating of teachers conditions to include 'a duty on teachers to take responsibility for their own professional development'; and OfSTED will be revising their school inspection criteria to include an inspection of the school's arrangements for the professional development of its staff. This will include the school's arrangements for identifying development needs, the extent to which these needs are reflected in the development opportunities undertaken and the impact the activities have on teacher effectiveness and pupil learning. In this one action, a rein-forcement of performance management, Investors in People and school self-evaluation is made clear. The review of Circular 4/98 com-pletes the picture, whereby initial teacher training providers will ensure trainees enter the profession with an understanding of their responsibility for their own professional development.

The issue of the school is taken up by Carol Adams, GTC (England) Chief Executive, in *A Professional Learning Framework* (2001), a set of guidelines on work-based learning. She says the framework will enable schools to explore options for professional development that are appropriate to their structures and circumstances. The learning framework is divided into eight sections: developing professional knowledge; engaging with research; engaging with professional net-works; developing your own professional profile; developing the learning community; professional involvement in the wider school and education agenda; learning through professional practice; and developing pedagogy in the context of information communication technology. Within these various elements there is a sign of the impor-tance of the relationship between teacher development and school development in any major CPD initiative. The school is the site for teacher learning, and this process of work-based learning is enhanced by collaboration among teachers and others in the school community and enhances the school as a learning community.

We have now reached a crisis in terms of the recruitment and reten-tion of teachers to the profession, with thousands of vacancies recorded in English schools and with some having to resort to the use of unqualified staff, four-day weeks and restrictions on curriculum access. At present the situation is less severe in Scotland but there are clear indications of major shortages looming in certain secondary school subjects while the availability of supply teachers for some local authorities is negligible. Such developments perhaps create a barrier to schools operating as 'learning organisations'. Nevertheless, the scene is set, therefore, for developing a much greater understanding across the profession of the importance of professional learning and the DfEE CPD strategy that promotes 'learning from each other . . . learning from what works' serves to underline the importance of work-based learning.

Conclusions

It is clear that the developments in the policy framework for performance management have been attenuated and bear witness to the deeply contested nature of performance management and to some of the underlying contradictions in the espoused purposes of the process: self-regulation and quality assurance as opposed to the ever-elaborating paranoia of quality control. Has there been a lack of emphasis on what it means to alter or improve performance rather than just identifying that weaknesses may exist? Our review of the developments associated with the concern with performance reinforces our belief that the relationship between performance management and improving professional practice is problematic.

The variety of different approaches to implementing programmes of CPD within the UK have been a response to the concern for improved performance and to the changing emphases in implementing a range of strategies that have sought to bring about change in schools. We seem to be at the point where we are beginning to formulate a more coherent understanding of the nature of CPD itself, which is founded on an understanding of the nature of teacher learning. The new CPD and performance management strategies (with their strong focus on improving professional practice through work-based learning initiatives) need to be understood by all actors in terms of the conceptualisation of CPD and of the relationship between teacher learning and school development throughout the UK.

The policy context is thus set fair for professional learning in school to take centre-stage and to build on existing good practices. Much CPD provision has been criticised over the years, whether school based, LEA provided or externally provided by university staff or other educational consultants. The Scottish Qualification for Headship (SQH) initiative, for example, has introduced formal work-based learning and partnerships between employers and higher education. For CPD qualifications this points the way ahead, as expectations of partnership and a recognition of school-based activity are evident while there is also a desire by many teachers to have higher education awards allied to enhanced professional status. A new paradigm may emerge, but the extent to which the current SQH 'delivery' model is economically sustainable when applied more widely to CPD provision becomes a key question.

We suggest that if professional practice is to be improved, development activity must involve work-based learning or school-based professional development. We argue that, despite the difficulties, work-based learning is the key that will unlock the potential of teacher CPD that will, in turn, produce the teachers and schools required of the twenty-first century.

The issues associated with managing centralised initiatives at school level and their potential overload on teachers and managers are clearly a concern to policy-makers and practitioners alike. The relationship between performance management and continuing professional development and the impact of these on raising the morale and status of the profession is complex; it requires careful and sensitive management at national, local and school level.

The emergence of the morale and status of the teaching profession as a policy concern has given rise to an alternative, which is to look to more tangible rewards for individual teachers through schemes of performance-related pay or progression-related pay, both to raise the morale overall and to create a view of the teaching profession as attractive to potential new entrants (as well as to maintain and improve the practice of serving teachers). This approach is more concerned with issues of motivation rather than the nature of teacher learning. We will focus on this area in the next chapter before returning to our discussion about teacher learning and the improvement of performance.

3

Changing rewards: performance-related pay

In this chapter we develop our views on the highly contested area of performance management systems in schools, on the debate surrounding performance-related pay (PRP) and on their relationship to managing and enhancing performance. This discussion is informed by recent evidence from the business context in the UK; the English Threshold Application processes in schools; the US models that make links with knowledge and skills-based reward systems; and the notion of School Achievement Awards and School-based Performance Awards in the UK and the USA.

The business context in the UK

In September 2000, Industry in Education (IIE), a national education trust supported by leading industrialists, produced a report entitled *Milestone or Millstone? Performance Management in Schools: Reflections on the Experiences of Industry'*. Its aim was to bring transferable experience of appraisal and performance management across to education in the context of the current debate on teachers' performance management procedures. The evidence presented, albeit from a small sample of ten business organisations, reflects the view that:

> Any notion that performance management is a concept 'past its sell-by date' is not true. In fact we found the very opposite to be the case, as did the Institute of Personnel and Development's [IPD's] research in 1997 which showed that 69% of organisations operate performance management. Of the 31% without a formal process, 48% planned to introduce one within 2 years (*ibid.*: 4).

These performance management processes in industry take a variety of forms and may or may not incorporate PRP; but, as the IPD's 1997 research shows, in addition to an overall growth in PRP, industry has also adopted a number of refinements, including competency-based pay and profit-related pay. The current performance management system being introduced by DfEE for English teachers, whereby progression beyond a certain level is linked to proven performance or ability, would apparently be seen as 'sound' by most of business organisations and by industry. It is described as a system of 'performance-related progression' rather than 'PRP' and is similar to some promotions available to professional staff in industry but without major changes of management responsibility. We are told that some business organisations use this approach for professional staff in addition to performance pay through bonuses or annually variable rewards.

All of which can appear to writer and reader as being a million miles away from the reality of schools and the constraints of school budgets. Yet, as the report reveals, specialist professional staff in business and industry have many job characteristics similar to teachers – in particular, where performance and rewards are not determined by simplistic financial or output measures. The IIE report is based on research in organisations where staff share common employment profiles and conditions such as the following:

- Professionally qualified and independent with expert skills, working with considerable autonomy in circumstances where success and failure cannot be measured by simple outputs;
- Under the management of a local unit which is broadly facilitative, rather than closely directive of their day to day work;
- Often leading experts in their fields with greater topic knowledge than anyone in their direct vertical line of management (IIE, 2000: 7).

This common ground with the education sector makes the themes emerging from the research valuable to the educational professional as the attempt is made to introduce the performance management process into English schools. It is probably important here to state the rationale provided in this 'business perspective', where performance management is described as: 'usually linked to the business planning cycle and is more to do with exploration and development than judgement. It is a means, rather than an end in itself. It facilitates open dialogue, personal professional development and commitment to quality in the workplace' (*ibid*.: 5).

Such a philosophy for performance management in schools could ensure the system supports those professional work-based learning processes that result in improved practices, as discussed in later chapters of this book. The findings of the IIE research are therefore discussed in relation to our main thesis that performance improves through the complex process of work-based learning, involving both the individual and other members of his or her working environment. It requires structure and support for this learning process to take place and involves the personal challenge of changing professional identity. Can a 'formal' performance management system and one related to pay or rewards help to promote such learning?

Personal and organisational gain

The IIE research found the following:

- Professional staff usually welcome feedback on their overall performance.
- People's 'values' generally include a need for some form of 'benefit' for high performance.
- A significant benefit for good performers arises from the existence of the feedback process itself – i.e. the awareness of doing, and being seen to be doing, a good job.

Leaving aside for the moment the notion of differentially valuing high performers over less well performing colleagues, there can be little doubt of the personal and organisational benefits of 'feedback on performance'. The importance of feedback to professional learning is highlighted in the discussion of assessing performance in this report. The major point we make as authors and professional developers is to emphasise the vital importance of skills development in the area of 'giving feedback to colleagues', if mentors, reviewers, appraisers or line managers are to contribute to real performance development.

Figure 3.1 identifies 'giving feedback to colleagues' amongst a range of vital and higher-order personal skills needed by manager and team leaders if the potential personal and organisational gains of appraisal and performance management are to be realised in schools.

An evolving process

All the organisations spoken to by IIE are constantly investing time and money to fine tune their performance management processes. In most organisations the need for long-term commitment and for the development of a 'culture of performance management' was stressed, rather than a once-off implementation of a paperwork-dominated scheme. Any cultural change takes time, and performance management therefore needs to be seen as part of a process of continuous

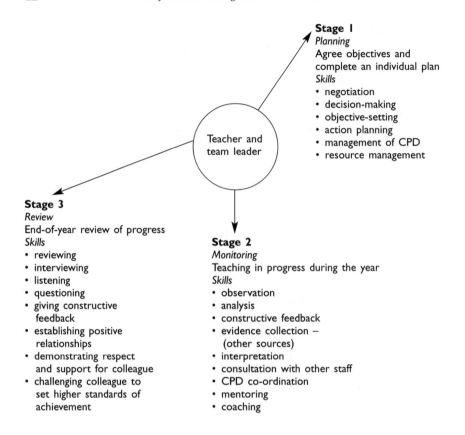

Stage 1
Planning
Agree objectives and
complete an individual plan
Skills
• negotiation
• decision-making
• objective-setting
• action planning
• management of CPD
• resource management

Teacher and
team leader

Stage 3
Review
End-of-year review of progress
Skills
• reviewing
• interviewing
• listening
• questioning
• giving constructive
  feedback
• establishing positive
  relationships
• demonstrating respect
  and support for colleague
• challenging colleague to
  set higher standards of
  achievement

Stage 2
Monitoring
Teaching in progress during the year
Skills
• observation
• analysis
• constructive feedback
• evidence collection –
  (other sources)
• interpretation
• consultation with other staff
• CPD co-ordination
• mentoring
• coaching

Figure 3.1 Performance management cycle and skills

improvement, linking individual and whole-school development. Work-based management development programmes, such as the Scottish Qualification for Headship (SQH) and the Leadership Programme for Serving Headteachers (LPSH) play an effective part in developing a continuous learning process of review and action planning, thus contributing to improvements in individual and organisational performance. However, as this book argues, developing the culture of continuing professional development (CPD) and giving teachers the skills and motivation to lock themselves into what Marker (2000) describes as a 'virtuous' cycle of critical review, planning, implementation and evaluation, requires a commitment by the government to address the attendant issues of resources – costs in staff time and the difficulties of providing appropriate development and support.

Setting objectives

Teachers in England have argued against the suitability of 'hard-edged' output-related objectives in the new teachers' appraisal and performance management framework. They maintain that pupil test and examination results cannot automatically measure good teaching. In industry, the IIE report reveals that objectives are set that combine individual with organisational ones – an approach championed by the Investors in People scheme. These objectives are usually a combination of 'results' and 'processes'.

The IIE report (2000: 8) goes on to argue that 'it would be difficult to argue that pupil achievement should have no place in a consideration of teacher performance'. However, viewing test and examination results as one source of contributory evidence does not, and should not, preclude the use of other indicators.

This interpretation supports the view that 'other indicators' may be comparative or normative and may take account of improvement against similar pupil cohorts elsewhere, or value-added in year-on-year tests and examination performance, rather than absolute results. It is worth reiterating that the DfEE's performance management framework uses the term 'pupil progress', which can clearly be interpreted in this more relative way. Indeed, as the performance management framework indicates, it is important that any planning discussions are based on an understanding of pupils' previous attainment. In the discussions between the teacher and manager, agreement is reached about how progress is measured and that the annual review should look at the assessment of progress.

It can be argued that one of the most interesting findings emerging from the IIE research into industry's experiences of performance management concerns this revelation that 'measures' are merely 'local understandings' and that it is possible to interpret the DfEE framework for performance management in this same way. The 'local understandings' and 'circumstances' are those that concern a particular professional's most important opportunities and challenges, developed in face-to-face dialogue between appraisee and appraiser. This philosophy supports the thesis running throughout this book that explores the importance of the cognitive and social processes of learning and improved performance. It also highlights again the crucial importance of the inter and intra-personal skills in use in the review of learning situations. We pick up this issue again in our concluding chapter.

External influences

The IIE report shows that, although teachers point out that their teaching results are largely dependent on external influences, many of which are beyond their control, this too is mirrored in each of the business organisations researched. These organisations stressed that the main way to manage the problem is to recognise the importance of external influences 'up front', with a stronger emphasis on the dialogue aspect of appraisal rather than communication of judgements through written systems. Most of the ten organisations interviewed had worked with their professional staff to find ways of measuring what was important for sustained high performance and to gain commitment to the process.

Their emphasis on high-quality dialogue, meaningful relationships and a shared commitment to examining quality performance is, of course, the hallmark of a learning community in action. It can be argued that the management development programmes such as SQH and LPSH (with their focus on rigorous individual and organisational analysis and detailed planning supported by expert tutoring and school-based mentor support) provides the structures that support such professional learning and development.

Making and valuing judgements

There is some concern in schools about senior teachers being required to make judgements about other teachers when performance management is fully implemented because they may not have the same level of expertise in the appraisee's subject. This concerns how a relatively non-expert individual can judge an expert's performance, and it raises the issue of the quality assurance of 'judgements'.

The IIE report reveals that an equivalent situation exists in industry. Some of those 'judged' were regarded as the top company specialists on their topics, or even world experts. However, this did not create undue problems in conducting appraisals, since relative non-expertise can be overcome by a discussion of the issues and agreed outputs or objectives. The report argues that the overall lesson from non-teaching sectors is that appraisal judgements can be carried out very effectively by managers whose training, management style and relationship with their staff are based on observations, questioning and monitoring of outputs rather than on 'I know the right way to do your job'.

Clearly there are implications here for high-quality training and development that focus on those important processes of change management which concern shared values and relationships building. The SQH training programmes, for example, requests candidates to be explicit about their professional values and to identify their strengths and areas for development in relation to a range of inter/intra-personal skills and abilities. This is vital to the development of a positive climate in school.

The IIE report (IEE, 2000: 9) claims that those working in situations where there are long-standing performance management arrangements in place 'would now complain if they did not receive regular feedback on their achievements and support in setting targets'. From this perspective, a core role of the line manager is to make judgements and to offer feedback and coaching to sustain or improve performance.

In education, we must continually question the stage of maturity reached by our schools in relation to the above assessment and human resource management skills. Evidence emerging from the LPSH programme shows that, of the 15 characteristics used to define highly effective heads, two are common weaknesses: 'holding people accountable' and 'developing potential in others'. This is a cause for concern and indicates the need for extended training requirements in the skills and processes underpinning effective performance management (see Figure 3.1). This concern is perhaps also exacerbated by the small amount of training provided through the Performance Management Consortia for the managers or team leaders in school. The DfEE courses are often instead 'information giving'.

The IIE report suggests much can be learnt from courses and training programmes run in industry in the performance management area. These place far greater emphasis on management style and interpersonal skills than on the mechanics of 'schemes'. Perhaps in education we need to recognise that our team leaders and many headteachers may have a shortfall in terms of their previous training in interpersonal management skills. They concentrate on the 'what' of performance management rather than on the complex human skills of making judgements and of communicating them constructively – the 'how'.

If we accept that the mature organisation concentrates on process, not form filling, then logic demands that training programmes for management development and school improvement do the same. The 'new' National Professional Qualification for Headship (NPQH) in England with its 'access' and 'development' stage of modules appears to have moved towards the 'process' of the work-based learning model espoused above, with its greater focus on a clear identification of a need and learning contract for school-based management development. However, the effects of a greater use of ICT-based learning, including online tutorials and 'hot-seats', need to be monitored closely in terms of their impact on the development of management style and interpersonal skills over a period of time. The NPQH candidate, like his or her Scottish counterpart on the SQH, is also very dependent on the quality of school-based tutoring and on access to management development experiences in school. Therefore, the quality of the headteacher's skills and understanding of the adult learning processes in schools is paramount in this professional learning model.

However, as Marker (2000) has recently discussed, there is a clear need to raise the quality of school-based assessment and professional development and the low level of support that exists in Scotland to bring about this improvement. Schools are 'thrown back too much on their own resources ... ideas and expertise' (*ibid*.: 923). In England, the 'judgement' and 'assessments' of teachers and headteachers against the threshold standards are externally assessed (validated) by nationally trained external assessors. This is a clear attempt to assure quality and consistency of standards across schools – but there is much debate about the subjectivity, level and interpretation of the threshold standards. Similarly, in England the nationally accredited roles of external advisers for headteacher review and performance management consultants are clear attempts to provide high-quality, consistent support and advice to schools. Unfortunately, many would claim this external support is insufficient and 'one off' whereas the development of effective appraisal and performance management skills and processes in school requires a more continuous relationship and investment in support and training.

Fair rewards

The IIE report (2000: 11) argues that 'Although it is only one aspect of performance management, if money dominates the debate, the result is that performance-related pay becomes the tail that wags the dog'. The authors of the IIE report observe that the debate on the DfEE green paper (1998) has, regrettably, tended to follow this course. They argue that the evidence from business shows that, whilst money is an important factor, 'other [significant] benefits' come from a performance management system, such as the attendant professional development training as well as the impact the system has on job satisfaction.

There has been much critical debate about the green paper and what some opponents see as a 'crude' linking of pay and performance.

Many might argue that the traditional pay scales are fairer in rewarding professionalism and experience than the new annual reviews of performance and incremental points which can be seen as divisive. However, as the IIE report (2000: 11) states, industry's experience reveals that 'reward based mainly on longevity of service is just as divisive and can act as a strong disincentive for younger staff'.

In practice, the DfEE performance management framework, it is claimed, is more akin to performance-linked progression rather than to a traditional PRP system. The IIE authors (*ibid.*) believe it is a long way from 'a return to a Victorian system of payment by results' (IEE, 2000: 10). At the time of writing this chapter, the authors would tend to agree with this interpretation, and the quiet incorporation of the performance management cycle philosophy into English schools would testify to its general acceptability in the profession. Besides which, the recruitment and retention teacher crisis in English schools has placed performance management into a more fluid and turbulent context than is desirable for its effectiveness.

It is perhaps regrettable that, in England, the national continuing professional development (CPD) strategy referred to earlier, which put teachers' entitlement to high-quality professional development centre-stage, was launched more than a year *after* the introduction of performance management in schools. This is a pity since the culture of the CPD strategy document with its subtitle 'Learning from each other . . . learning from what works' reinforces the main messages (within this book) of the central importance of work-based learning and the sharing of good practices. Indeed, the annual appraisal cycle and review meeting formalises the value of learning from each other in a situation where the participants can talk openly, share information and exchange good practice. The two initiatives of performance management and CPD clearly go hand in hand and are being led strongly by the DfEE, with an emphasis on individual and whole-school learning. There is a huge dependency built into both initiatives for headteachers to manage the systems fairly and effectively for all staff if they are to succeed in the longer term. Tomlinson has argued for improvements in training in PRP appraisal, proper monitoring of it, continuous but selective assessment for teachers, evaluation of *all* school jobs, and payment on the basis of discretion exercised. Instead, the training, monitoring, assessment and job evaluation skills of the profession currently remain relatively underdeveloped. LEAs have no automatic role in supporting and improving these skills and processes and time will tell whether, as Tomlinson argued, the green paper must count as an opportunity missed.

Rewarding individuals or teamwork?

This is an interesting section in the IIE report where the assumption that teaching is a 'team activity' is challenged by a comparison with industry's experiences. If the commonly held view of the teaching profession, by the profession, is that teaching is a team activity, then a logical corollary might be the belief that individual performance-linked rewards are divisive for other members of the team.

The report (IIE, 2000: 11) suggests the following business or industry definition of a team: 'A small number of people with complementary skills who are committed to a common purpose, performance goals and approach, for which they hold themselves mutually accountable.' It goes on (*ibid.*) to argue that whilst teachers have a 'common purpose', this is often manifest as a 'collective influence on outcomes, rather than as an interdependent team working together on the delivery process'. Indeed, the report claims that some teachers, with this 'singular accountability in the classroom', fit the definition of team working less well than many professionals in the outside world.

Furthermore, in industry, interdependent team performance has not prevented differential individual rewards being made. Instead, the IIE's experience has found that it is more a case of 'fine-tuning the balance of personal recognition and team recognition to best motivate individuals who can make the largest team contribution' (*ibid.*). Certainly, this last statement reveals the importance of line managers, team leaders and headteachers *knowing* and *diagnosing* the capacity of their staff and their individual contributions, strengths and areas for further development. It captures the crucial role of management in ensuring this 'balancing act' of reward, motivation and further development is maintained for the benefit of individuals, the team and the whole school.

Interestingly, the English, Welsh and Scottish national programmes for management development all promote the capacity to work well in a team, as well as leading a team, as important 'personal attributes'. In these programmes therefore teamwork is being seen to be rewarded (through assessment and accreditation measures) in *individual* performance terms. As such, therefore, an individual performance management development objective can help to drive cultural changes in schools focused on building collaboration and teamwork.

The introduction of individual performance management does not exclude the possibility of a system of team-based rewards, and the School Achievement Award, introduced in the green paper, is an example of this in practice (see below). The IIE report properly notes the fact that most teams in school include support staff and that business would see recognising 'staff' as meaning 'all staff' as essential in the pursuit of managing whole-school development and cultural change through performance management. Indeed, achieving the Investors in People award promoted in the recent DfEE 'CPD Strategy for Teaching and Learning' (2001) requires this focus on *all staff.*

Disconnecting appraisal and pay discussions

The IIE report (2000) reveals how, in industry, the appraisal process has evolved over the last 10–15 years and how many companies now use it to 'put greater emphasis on future aims, objectives, challenges and development actions [rather] than on looking back to judge or explain past performance' (IEE, 2000: 11). The report also claims that appraisal is commonly used in industry to discuss training and development needs and to consider wider career aspirations as well as challenges in current posts. As part of the performance management cycle in schools, this is good practice for the emergent annual appraisal/review meetings to emulate – but this is very dependent for its effectiveness on the management skills of the team leaders and headteachers involved in the process. In industry, this developmental emphasis is often signalled by a change of name for the process and the term 'appraisal' is not often used since it carries too much association with more backward-looking, judgemental schemes. In education, it can be argued that this association does not necessarily exist; indeed, if the HMI/OfSTED report of 1996 is to be regarded as reliable evidence of practice and perceptions, then schoolteacher (and headteacher) appraisal schemes seriously lacked the 'judgemental' characteristic and were criticised for their developmental and 'cozy' approaches to the process.

The IIE report does not discount the inevitable connection between performance management and pay; it simply reveals that UK companies have found it helpful to separate the discussion of the two issues since there can be 'a conflict of aims' when the two are dealt with together. For example, in some businesses there is a separation of performance reviews (mid-year) and pay reviews (year-end). It can be argued that the recent threshold assessments in England have been introduced in the same way – that is, quite separately and in advance of the more developmental performance management and annual appraisal processes that were launched in the summer of 2000.

The threshold standards and the system of progression into a higher pay range they signify would, it is claimed, be seen as 'sound' by most of business and industry. This system of compiling evidence of performance across previous years supports the importance of creating an 'appraisal history', since entry to a new salary range should not be determined by an impressive single year's performance. This 'performance-related progression', it is claimed by the IIE, is similar to some promotions available to professional staff in industry that do not include major changes of management responsibility. The Secretary of State has also described threshold assessment as 'performance-related promotion', whilst others might see it as a 'standards-based pay system'.

What is clear is that nearly 200,000 of the approximately 250,000 teachers who could have applied have done so. What is not clear at this stage is why 50,000 eligible teachers did not apply and whether the reasons were associated with a lack of time, an inability to present sufficient evidence to meet the standards or out of principle. Issues emerging from the Cambridge Educational Institute's database, however, reveal the crucial importance of effective leadership and management of the threshold process in schools and the huge variations in the support provided for teachers from senior managers in this part of the performance management cycle. There are clearly indicators here of the training and development needs of headteachers and line managers, especially in the challenging skills of supporting teachers' own assessment of performance, evidence collection and review processes (see Figure 3.1). It is argued that the one-day conferences for headteachers provide little more than information on managing the cycle of performance management in school; they do not attempt to develop the human resource management skills of headteachers. Neither is this national training targeted at team leader skills development, unless the headteacher identifies this as an area for development in follow-up school-based training sessions.

The emergent USA model – knowledge and skills-based pay

We move now away from a consideration of the experiences of performance management and PRP/progression in the UK business context – and its relevance to schools – to a discussion of developments in 'teacher compensation' in districts and states throughout the USA. The main source of the discussion is the definitive book by Odden and Kelly (1997), which explored alternative forms of teacher compensation, and Odden's more recent article (2000), in which he argues that new and better forms of teacher compensation are desirable. At the time of writing, there is no comparable research published on the UK's limited experiences in this field. Odden and Kelly have been able to develop a breadth of understanding that enables them to conceptualise alternative models of teacher compensation due to the range of developments in practice across the USA.

Odden (2000) is now making clear proposals for a system of teacher pay that simultaneously enhances teaching as a profession and also reinforces the goals and strategies of standards-based educational reform. He proposes a new teacher salary structure that ties in salary increases to take account of the acquisition of new knowledge and skills. He rejects merit-pay based on its 'subjective judgements of administrators' and promotes the use of 'professional benchmarks' as tools for assessing the knowledge and skills of teachers at key points in their careers. As such, Odden's assertions can be seen to have relevance to England, where the use of national standards at QTS, Threshold, Advanced Skills Teacher and Headteacher (NPQH) levels are already an accepted part of a national assessment of performance 'scheme'. Additionally, as we have noted, the McCrone agreement in Scotland can be interpreted as an acceptance that 'professional benchmarks', once achieved, should lead to increased salary.

Odden (*ibid.*) suggests there are a number of reasons why teacher compensation can now move forward in America:

- The National Board for Professional Teaching Standards (NBPTS) has a process for the certification of accomplished teachers. Any payment for achieving these standards would be based on a knowledge and skills-based rewards system.
- New private sector compensation models provide alternative models for schools to consider. These include knowledge and skills-based pay, competency pay, group-based performance awards and gain-sharing. All these models allow companies to reward employees on the basis of skills and expertise rather than experience, and to provide group bonuses when work teams contribute to improvements in organisational performance.
- The National Commission on Teaching and America's Future recommended pay increases on the basis of teachers' knowledge and skills (as well as incentives for improved performance) as one of several strategies for enhancing teaching as a profession.

Odden and Kelly (1997) argued that a new compensation structure for teachers is essential. They believe it could reinforce those elements that intrinsically motivate teachers, such as learning new teaching and management skills and being successful in raising student achievement. Odden's (2000) assertions are basically that there are now the tools for assessing the knowledge and skills of beginning teachers available for use by the profession. These include the Educational Testing Service (ETS), the PRAXIS Series, the Council of Chief State School Officers (CCSS) and the Interstate New Teacher Assessment and Support Consortium (INTASC). Furthermore, there are tools for assessing the knowledge and skills of experienced teachers developed by the NBPTS and, more recently, ETS has developed an intermediate means for assessing 'mid-career' teachers.

Kerchner and Elwell (2000) confirm much of this analysis whilst discussing the importance of teacher unions in ensuring fairness and substantive and procedural justice, and they suggest a much broader redefined role for the unions in the USA. They argue it is important to make clear the distinctions between rewards and incentives in improving the appeal of teaching as a profession.

Clearly there is much of value to debate in these American experiences and parallel developments in the UK, especially in the use of national standards for the assessment of the knowledge and skills levels of beginning and experienced teachers and aspiring headteachers. The further development and use of a national standards framework, linked to planned professional development and the portfolio collection of evidence of achievement, is a major plank in the DfEE's national strategy for CPD (2001b) and a similar approach likely to be adopted in Scotland.

Odden (2000) argued that, besides the individual teacher assessment of knowledge and skills, the school-based achievement or performance awards should also contribute to teachers' pay. The next section examines the motivational potential of such whole-school or group awards of pay to improve teacher and manager performance in schools.

School-based achievement and performance awards – emergent English and USA experiences

School Achievement Awards (England)

This element of the DfEE's performance and reward strategy focuses on the 'whole-school' team and in this respect can be seen to balance the individual nature of threshold payments. Over 30 per cent of schools have recently been notified of their success in achieving a 'School Achievement Award' from the Secretary of State.

Three quarters of the awards have been made to schools that have improved faster than average over the last three years. A quarter of the awards have been made to schools whose results in a single year were particularly good compared with other schools in similar circumstances, based on the proportion of pupils eligible for free school meals. Amounts received by schools have been approximately £5,000 for a typical 200-pupil school and £30,000 for a typical 1,000-pupil school. Individual bonuses for staff (i.e. *all* staff, not just teachers) are therefore significant, and governors will need to ensure a sensitive and fair management of the allocation of the award to all staff in school if the motivational benefits of the award are to be achieved.

Evidence from the USA

The equivalent of School Achievement Awards in the USA are the School-Based Performance Awards (SBPA). There appears to be good evidence from the USA that they are effective in motivating school staff to improve performance and, if given acceptable criteria, are recognised as fair. The Consortium for Policy Research in Education (CPRE) at the University of Wisconsin, Madison, has amassed an enormous amount of information on the design and administration of SBPAs in states across the USA.

Three pieces of research are worth examining here. First, research in Kentucky suggests that if teachers believe that through their efforts they can meet the student performance goals of the SBPA programme, and if they believe the performance goals will result in a reward that is meaningful to them, they will modify teaching strategies and levels of effort to improve student performance. Secondly, research exploring teacher attitudes to teacher bonuses awarded under SPBA schemes in Kentucky and Charlotte-Macklenburg showed that the possibility of earning bonuses has a strong motivational potential. Furthermore, bonuses were seen to be not only desirable but also consistent with other extrinsic and intrinsic outcomes associated with attaining student achievement goals.

However, without careful planning, design and administration to ensure fairness, the high motivational potential of SBPAs can remain unrealised. A third research paper from CPRE addresses these design issues, which are briefly summarised below:

- The importance of using multiple performance measures across academic and non-academic dimensions of school performance.
- The need for clarity and fairness in calculating the desired change or improvement, using standard and value-added models.

- Ensuring the level of challenge is reasonable. Unrealistic and unattainable goals will have a negative influence.
- The need for clarity in terms of who should receive the award, how many award levels there should be and how large the awards should be.
- The need for guaranteed funding.
- The importance of enabling conditions and support for the SBPA programme – there are three types of enablers: teacher knowledge, skills, abilities; teaching methods and techniques; and school climate.
- The need to evaluate the consequences of the SBPA programme, including whether teaching strategies actually change and improve.

The USA experience of SBPA appears to indicate that the programmes and bonuses for groups of teachers have a focusing effect on teaching practices, resource alignment, collaboration and teamwork. Teachers understood the programme goals and were committed to them. Those whose expected bonus values and other positive outcomes were higher reported more clarity and commitment to the goals. In the Pennsylvania district teachers could expect to earn up to \$2,000 on a group bonus and \$2,700 for individual performance.

In sum, the early research evidence from US experiences (whether in relation to SBPA programmes or to knowledge and skills-based pay programmes) indicates the vital importance of effective communication and the involvement of all staff in the processes. The performance targets should be meaningful but attainable (an appropriate 'reach'), and the programme itself must be part of an overall school improvement or educational reform system, not 'bolt on'. It would seem logical to suggest that this research and evaluation evidence from the USA might be used to help evaluate the performance management system and the School Achievement Awards introduced in England over the last 12 months or so.

Conclusion

This chapter has considered the new culture of performance management and annual appraisal through an examination of the wider business application of these processes, as reported through the IIE. The discussion has raised both the potential gains for the teaching profession as well as the challenges and potentially 'lost opportunities' in the teachers' green paper through a lack of continuous high-quality support and training, particularly for team leaders and managers in schools.

The discussion of PRP, focused on the importance of placing 'pay' into the wider context of job satisfaction and career development and suggested that the DfEE performance management system is instead a more ambiguous system of 'performance-linked progression'. At the time of writing, the impact of annual appraisal and reviews of performance against clear objectives and standards is yet to bite in schools. The context of the recruitment and retention crisis in the profession, together with the flexible contractual arrangements made possible through Education Action Zone and City Academy Status, can be seen to be moving the discussion of teachers' pay as related to performance into more diverse and locally agreed arenas.

The main thrust of this chapter has been to identify the importance of supporting and developing the skills of teachers, team leaders and managers in the challenging areas of appraisal, assessment of performance and review. The changing context of 'diversity' in schools, as well as the issue of whole-school or team achievement awards for performance, accentuates this urgent need to support the development of rigorous self-evaluation and assessment skills across the profession that, together with access to high-quality professional development and training, must lead to the raising of standards of achievement in schools.

4

Changing professional practice

Introduction

Earlier in this book we surveyed the policy contexts in which current approaches to performance management have emerged, with their emphasis on establishing structures at service, school and individual levels that will ensure, first, clarity in the description of roles, tasks and targets and, secondly, the means for ensuring these are undertaken. The implication of all this is that the performance of individual teachers will be improved, which is all very well but, as we signalled in Chapter 1, if we are to enhance professional performance it is important to think about what is entailed in changing it. How professional development opportunities are planned and provided should be based on an understanding of what improving practice means, both for individuals and for the organisations in which they work. This remains, at the end of reading all the policy documents, an extremely murky area full of interesting contradictions. In this chapter we will attempt to clarify this issue of professional learning.

Fullan (1991: 36) proposed in the *New Meaning of Educational Change* that 'Ultimately the transformation of subjective realities is the essence of change'. On this basis it is how practitioners make sense of their work, how they perceive their role and their professional identity that determine their practice. Any attempt at improving teachers' performance, therefore, depends upon influencing the sense-making processes they rely on in undertaking their work. This process of making sense of change as a basis for adopting new practices involves thinking and feeling as well as acquiring new skills and behaviours. With its links to professional identity it is also embedded within the social context of the school, so that relationships with colleagues and pupils have an important part to play in determining its course and its outcomes.

The parameters of change

Extent of change

There is obviously a range of possible changes individuals can make that will affect the way in which they carry out their work. Depending on the nature of the change, improving practice might involve relatively little new learning or the acquisition of a substantial number of new capabilities for any given individual. At one end of the scale it may be that people want to extend their skills and knowledge in ways that are largely compatible with their present practice and, therefore, require only very minor alterations in their behaviour. At the other extreme, practitioners may want (or have) to move into areas of work that require a far more substantial set of changes on their part. The nature and extent of the learning the person needs to undertake are thus dependent on the content and context of the desired change.

However, content is not the only variable. People's responses to the same learning task can vary quite markedly. For example, if I see myself as reasonably computer literate, learning how to use email merely involves the acquisition of some new knowledge and an adjustment of current skills. The new learning can be accommodated quite easily within the framework of my current capabilities and self-identity. On the other hand, if I have no confidence at all in my ability to use a computer, learning how to use email successfully may require a much more fundamental change on my part. In this case I am going to have to change my attitudes and feelings about computers and my capacity to use technology, in addition to knowing about email and developing the specific skills required to use it.

Mindful of this combination of the content of the learning and the learner's perception of the development task, the categories outlined by Hatch (1997) as a means of conceptualising cultural change provide a useful framework for thinking about development needs:

- *Absorption*   The new learning can simply slot into the current frames of reference of learners.
- *Accommodation*   The new learning will require the learners to stretch, adapt or alter parts of their frames of reference.
- *Revolution*   The new learning requires a radical alteration of the learners' frames of reference.

Most learning that leads to significant change in practice is going to fall into the second category, occasionally the third. In either case, the underlying assumptions, values and beliefs that make up the person's professional identity and his or her framework for interpreting his or her working environment will need to change if the acquisition of new knowledge and skills is to serve a practical purpose (Joyce and Showers, 1988).

Effort associated with change

Other factors to consider in planning professional development are commitment and the emotional aspects of change. Where improving performance entails simple absorption, learners do not need to sustain a huge amount of effort to achieve their goals. Once they move beyond absorption into the area of *accommodation* or *revolution*, learners will require increasingly greater commitment and effort in order to change their practice successfully, and the process is more likely to generate feelings of discomfort and unease. This is not simply because of the need to learn new ways of operating but also because 'old' patterns of meaning and behaviour will have to be replaced to allow for the adoption of new practice (Marris, 1986). A current example of this might be teachers' involvement in their school being recognised as 'health-promoting'. For some this will challenge their assumptions about their role as a teacher and their beliefs about the purpose of schooling. These frameworks of belief will have to change to accommodate the idea this is a valuable and worthwhile innovation if their practice is going to alter, and this may well arouse quite strong feelings.

The effects on learners of having to reject or modify current assumptions and behaviour are particularly strong in continuing professional development (CPD). As established practitioners, many of the learners will already have invested heavily in pursuing certain values and in establishing habits of practice they rely upon. As these teachers change their ideas and begin to alter their practice, they are likely to experience a loss of competence prior to establishing and integrating new skills and habits into their repertoire (Drummond and McLaughlin, 1994). Eraut (1994: 360) typifies some of the problems substantive change can bring:

> Much INSET . . . is concerned with teaching processes rather than, or in addition to, changes in content . . . I would like to draw attention once again to the problem of unlearning or abandoning existing practices and routines. Changing one's teaching style involves de-skilling, risk, information overload and mental strain as more and more gets treated as problematic and less and less is taken for granted.

Obviously this is not the only side to learning; excitement, growth and pleasure in increasing capability are also part of the experience.

However, the deconstruction of previous practice presents a very real problem for learners. Sources of personal and professional support during the process will be important in helping them to persist and work through this stage of the learning process.

Experiencing influencing change

Lastly, there is the issue of what type of experiences will support the kinds of 'changes of mind' we have outlined and that will also enable practitioners to put into practice the behaviours that support their new insights. Certainly the feedback on the customary diet of CPD is not particularly encouraging in this regard (Joyce and Showers, 1988).

There are a number of models for provision. The traditional technical-rational model of professional training is organised on a hierarchy of knowledge that starts with the 'scientific' basis for practice followed by the input of procedural or applied knowledge after which, with some period of supervision to develop his or her own practical knowledge of the craft, the person is ready to practise. This model favours theoretical knowledge over experiential learning.

This hierarchical, or linear, model of learning, has been further elaborated, for example, by Joyce and Showers (*ibid.*), who based their proposed programme for teacher development on research into the establishment of new practices in the classroom. They argue that, without follow-up work in schools to provide feedback and support to teachers as they implemented new practice, there was little transfer of learning. This was the case even where staff development programmes supplemented teaching input with opportunities for discussion and workshops to practise new behaviours. Their extension of the didactic model has the advantage of placing a much stronger emphasis on the importance of the workplace as a site for learning.

However, whether such a model represents the reality of professional learning is open to question. It certainly does not match with the action learning/research cycle that represents an alternative model based on the notion of experiential learning. The iterative approach underpinning this cycle could well be more effective and certainly more nearly resembles the conditions for learning that are most constantly available to established practitioners. There is the advantage in the repeating spiral of action research of tying practice and theorising very closely together, thus increasing the chances, through immediacy of use, of the adoption/adaptation of theoretical ideas that are relevant to the practitioner's problems in the field.

To summarise, an essential target for planned professional development has to be perceptual change involving both thinking and feeling about the nature and purpose of professional work. It is only through changing their perceptual frameworks that learners can extend and expand the meaning of their practice and, hence, feel it is worth while making the effort to alter what they do. In this sense the key to improving performance becomes supporting successfully a process of 'sense-making' by teachers that will make new practices professionally meaningful and valuable to them at the same time as providing them with opportunities to acquire appropriate skills and knowledge.

Making sense

There are two common ways of delineating sense-making processes, one of which is concerned with the underlying perceptual frameworks people develop in order to interpret their world. This work draws on comparative studies of reasoning processes in different individuals (Piaget, 1954; Vygotsky, 1962; Bruner, 1966). The other, which is less familiar, centres on the notion of identity and sees this as the key construct in determining perception and action. Thus making sense of changes in practice can be thought of as involving changes in individuals' ways of interpreting

- the environment and their practice; and
- the self.

Whilst this is not a clear-cut distinction it is worth making because it points to important elements of the learning process. Before going on to look at the learning processes that will help people to reinterpret these two structures, it is worth exploring the categories a little further.

Interpreting the environment and practice

In the cognitive field, sense-making is seen as a core professional ability. Many writers have pointed out that the claim to professionalism is based on the ability to apply expertise to the solution of problematic issues (Schon, 1983; Eraut, 1994; Boud and Feletti, 1997). This requires the capability to make sense of issues, to select the relevant features of the context and to make decisions about the best way forward. As Tripp (1993: 7) remarks, 'sound judgement is what we value professionals for', which puts the ability to make sense at the heart of professional practice. A number of research studies have shown that this capability is a key component in superior performance: 'at the lowest level the novice learner has dispersed knowledge; list like knowledge of isolated facts with little conceptual integration. More advanced learners possess "elaborated knowledge" ... richly organised to support use in the solving of clinical problems' (Swanson *et al.*, 1994: 273). Likewise in the field of school leadership, the capacity to formulate and communicate a shared vision for the school is seen as a crucial capability. This 'purposing of the organisation' is seen as one of the key practices of effective leaders in many fields (Vaill, 1996). Lack of attention to sense-making and clarifying values and 'vision' in the education of school leaders has deleterious effects on the development of their practice:

> many current school leaders are unable to develop such consistency [of direction in relation to their day-to-day decisions], most likely, we believe, because they do not have a set of goals, values and vision for their staff and schools clearly formulated ... in their own minds (Leithwood *et al.*, 1992: 54).

Leithwood and his team (*ibid.*) compared the way in which expert and novice headteachers approached their work. The most significant differences in solving professional problems were based on the following three characteristics:

1) *Solution processes*   Expert school leaders exhibited better planning, taking more care to be clear about the strategy to be adopted and to work through the various stages of the process. They took better account of contingencies and predicted likely constraints more accurately. They were much more likely to monitor implementation.
2) *Interpretation*   Experts collected a wider range of data and spent longer over this stage of problem-solving. They actively sought the opinions of others and were far more likely to take account of prevailing professional judgement. They articulated and tested assumptions.
3) *Goals, principles and values*   Experts were better able to articulate these clearly and subjected them to scrutiny. They were also able to prioritise key issues in this regard (adapted from Leithwood *et al.*, *ibid.*: 77).

This is an interesting list in that it points to the most marked difference between novice and expert headteachers as lying in the technical skills of implementation but that this difference is underpinned by two 'invisible' cognitive skills:

1) Being able to pay attention to a fuller range of data and analyse it in a more sophisticated and holistic manner.
2) Having a clearer and more considered awareness of principles and purpose.

The importance of cognitive structures in developing expertise links to the notion that expert practitioners understand their practice at a meta-cognitive level and that this is what gives them mastery over their performance (Rogers, 1983). The key to this is developing practice to the point where the principles on which it is based are well understood. Once this is achieved the practitioner is no longer confined to repeating actions that have already been learned but can invent new practice by applying principles to new contexts:

> In perceiving some of our own acts in a generalising fashion we isolate them from our total mental activity and are thus able to focus on this process as such and to enter into a new relationship to it. In this way, becoming conscious of our operation and viewing it as of a certain kind leads to its mastery (Vygotsky, 1962: 91–92).

Excellent practice, whether in management or teaching, thus requires an integration of strategic and operational thinking where practitioners have an awareness of the purpose, values and understanding that underpin how they carry out their work. It is this deep understanding that 'enables flexible and appropriate use of the behaviour in multiple situations and prevents the often ludicrous following of "recipes" for teaching' (Joyce and Showers, 1988: 74). However, our analysis so far is only a partial explanation of changing performance in that it treats change as largely a matter for the individual. Real change in the professional practice of individuals can only take place in their working environment. It can only take place in interaction with others. Sense-making in terms of professional identity and defining the nature of one's role is essentially a social process (Weick, 1995).

Interpreting the self

One key feature of substantive alterations in professional performance is that these cannot be separated from some change in the learner's perception of his or her professional identity (Taylor, 1997). As Leithwood *et al.* (1992: 12) point out in relation to school headteachers: 'What school leaders do is most directly a consequence of what they think. School leaders have been observed to engage in quite distinct patterns of practice shaped by how they think about their work.' This links with work in the field of cultural psychology, where individuals are seen as continuously engaging in a process of sense-making that is both individual and collective. The key drivers in this process are each individual's need for:

Self-enhancement	seeking and maintaining a positive view and feeling about oneself;
Self-efficacy	seeing oneself as competent and effective;
Self-consistency	sensing and experiencing oneself as consistent, and having a continuity of identity (Weick, 1995: 20).

These needs are met, or denied, by the way in which the person experiences interactions with others, which either affirm or undermine his or her sense of self.

Since any desired improvement in a teacher's practice only becomes operational in the social context of the school and the classroom, colleagues and pupils have a crucial influence on implementation (and adoption). For example, if I go on a course and learn skills for using positive approaches to behaviour management in my classroom, when I return to school I am far less likely to be successful in maintaining and extending my new practice if my headteacher, colleagues and pupils regard positive behaviour management with scepticism. Given this lack of support I have the choice of three positions (Burr, 1995):

1) Accepting the construction of others, denying the worth of the course and not attempting to implement the practice.
2) Appearing to comply with their views but trying to implement the practice in my own classes and trying to persuade them differently over time.
3) Actively opposing their views and perhaps being forced to take up a fixed and contrary position.

The first course is the easiest to adopt, the second may well prove very difficult to sustain and the third is clearly risky. Under these circumstances it is not unsurprising that attending courses often has little long-term effect on practice.

One of the difficulties with many programmes for staff development is that providers have not necessarily seen professional change as socially constructed and, therefore, have not recognised that the development of the individual and the organisation should not be treated separately (Dadds, 1994). The issue of matching individual development needs to school development needs is not simply a matter of supporting the development of the school at the possible expense of the individual. It embodies a basic truth about practice. Professional learning is essentially interactive and involves both practitioners *and* the people they work with (Eraut, 1994: 35).

On the basis of this analysis, any intervention to improve performance must go beyond a simple delineation of skills, abilities and knowledge. It must recognise that:

- understanding, assumptions, beliefs and values play a crucial part in determining practice;
- changing practice substantively involves some change in professional identity; and
- practice is socially constructed and maintained, and new learning on the part of one individual depends on the learning of others in the same work environment.

We should therefore be very wary of definitions of professional competence that are confined to a concentration on behaviour and of notions that professional development is simply a matter of spreading good practice (Barber and Sebba, 1999). The danger of mimicry is that teachers' thinking is confined to a narrow operational level that is inadequate to support the development of a repertoire of adaptable behaviours. Such forms of learning will not enable practitioners to meet the variety of needs they are likely to confront in the future (Barnett, 1994; Fielding, 1999).

Sense-making is a very complex process and it may be useful at this stage to explore how it takes place in rather more detail. In order to do this we will consider the issues under two main headings:

1) The reflective learning process – cognitive change linked to practice.
2) The social learning process – cultural change linked to practice.

The reflective learning process

Within education the starting point for this approach is traceable to Dewey's (1938) concept of experiential learning and his identification of reflection as a crucial part of the process. Reflection occurs when people experience a mental irritant, a puzzle, a query. They then seek to find a means of resolving the issue through a process of active inquiry.

Schon (1983: 39–42) later refined this idea by linking it to action and he used it as a basis for developing the notion of reflective practice.

He felt that the view of professionalism as the rational application of scientific knowledge had outlived its usefulness. A model of professional practice that allowed for greater flexibility, responsiveness to others and adaptability was required in confronting the increasingly complex crises of contemporary society.

For Schon, solving problems, once they have been identified, is a technical matter. However, forming problems is a more sophisticated task that involves values in the selection of frames of interpretation. Increasingly, problem-forming is an essential activity for professionals, as one of Schon's colleagues graphically pointed out:

> What decision makers deal with, I maintain, are messes not problems ... A mess is a system of external conditions that produces dissatisfaction. It can be conceptualised as a system of problems in the same sense in which a physical body can be conceptualised as a system of atoms (Ackoff, 1980: 29).

Developing the capacity to frame problems out of these 'messes' requires professionals to become reflective practitioners actively engaged in extending their own procedural theory through reflection in action. Schon believes this happens when, in the course of action, something arises that makes practitioners pause and turn their thought back on the action to try to form the problem and resolve it. Central to this process is developing an awareness of the self as an actor in both a technical and an ethical sense in order to make a judgement on the worth of a particular action.

One important aspect of Schon's approach is his affirmation of knowledge creation and theory-making on the part of the practitioner. In this sense he does not support the traditional view of professionalism as the application of scientific knowledge to the concerns of clients. Schon believes the role of the professional has fundamentally altered. In an age where goals and purposes are frequently contested and where the most pressing problems are so complex as to defy solution through a technical-rational approach, there is a need for a new kind of professionalism. This new professionalism needs to align itself more with concepts of artistry and design where the practitioner works with the client to achieve a 'desirable future' rather than acting as a source of 'authoritative solutions' to the client's problems (Schon, 1983: 300).

Within the literature there is a general agreement that the reflective process consists of practitioners examining their actions using both evidence from the field and the ideas of others. The outcome of this process is the further development of the practitioner's own theory

Technical	Practical judgement Diagnostic judgement	What do I do here and now? Did I make the right practical judgement?
Ethical	Reflective judgement Critical judgement	Did I act according to my beliefs and values? Are my beliefs and values defensible?

Figure 4.1   Types of professional judgement
Source: Adapted from Tripp (1993: 140)

as to what makes for good practice in context. This is then applied and the evaluation of the results leads to new insights that start the next cycle of this learning process (Kolb, 1984). This reflective examination of practice has two basic focuses: the technical aspects and the ethical aspects of the case. Tripp's (1993) idea of four types of professional judgement about practice helps to extend these concepts (see Figure 4.1).

Schon's analysis points to three essential elements in developing this reflective process:

1) An action research cycle based on Lewin's (1952) idea of deliberate experimentation with practice in context as a means of enhancing professional performance.
2) A process of personal examination that focuses on intention and purpose in serving the interests of the client.
3) Systems of appreciation and a language as tools for reflection.

These three are inextricably linked because self-examination of practice is part of the action research cycle and this examination cannot take place if practitioners do not have a language and concepts for analysing and critiquing their actions.

One way of representing the reflective process is as a two-way interactive relationship between theory and practice. Figure 4.2 illustrates two phases of theorising in and on action. The first is the formulation of theory by engaging in the kinds of operations listed in the upper box: description, analysis, reflection, explanation, critique. These cognitive operations are very familiar as the target of many traditional academic courses, although they are not usually linked directly to the practitioner's own actions. The second stage of the process attracts less attention in the literature and teacher education but is equally crucial. This is the move from theory back into practice involving the operations listed in the lower box in Figure 4.2: application, translation, interpretation. This stage is often left to the practitioners on the grounds that, once they understand the theory, it will be a relatively

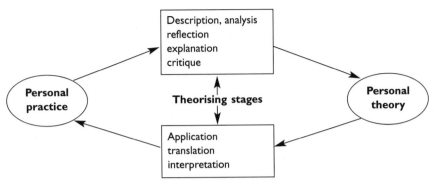

Figure 4.2 Interactive relationship of practice and theory
Source: Adapted from Tripp (1993: 150)

straightforward matter to put it into practice. Complaints about the efficacy of courses that neglect this stage of learning indicate this is a mistaken assumption for many learners. The implication for any programme of professional development is that the learner needs to be involved in activities and processes that will enable these two sets of cognitive operations to occur.

A learning programme may successfully extend and develop various frames of meaning for the practitioner but still not have an impact on practice. The models for reflective learning we have outlined imply it is not sufficient to develop someone's theoretical knowledge and understanding if this does not connect with his or her procedural framework (Argyris and Schon, 1974). To improve performance the learner needs to develop:

- the interconnections between relevant frameworks of meaning;
- an awareness of the dynamic interaction between these frameworks; and
- the ability actively to use this dynamic for him or herself.

The more holistic and consistent the overall frames of reference developed by students, the better equipped they will be to enhance their professional expertise. The connections that need to be developed are shown in Figure 4.3.

The social learning process

In exploring this process we are relying on the work of those psychologists (Vygotsky, 1978; Potter and Wetherall, 1987) who have developed a 'social constructionist' approach to explaining why

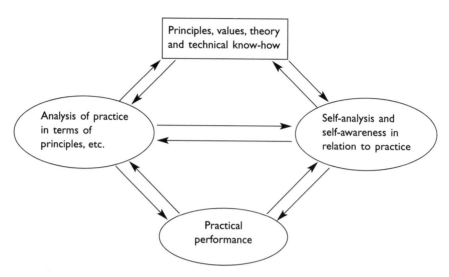

Figure 4.3   Linking the different schemas

humans act as they do. The link to sense-making is clear in the definition given by Gergen (1985): 'Social constructionism is principally concerned with elucidating the processes by which people come to describe, explain, or otherwise account for the world in which they live' (cited in Edwards, 1997: 78). The meaning people make of their world and their role within it is largely determined by the way these are commonly interpreted by those they interact with.

The key role of social processes in sense-making rests on evidence from investigations in social and organisational psychology. One of the important contexts for the fulfilment of the individual's basic need for affiliation (friendship, support, love and affection) was the workplace. Groups at work are seen as 'a primary means of developing, enhancing, and confirming our sense of identity and maintaining our self-esteem' (Schein, 1980: 150). The various groups that impinge on the individual are a means of establishing the social norms of the work context for that person. They enable individuals to shape their behaviour in order to gain and maintain approval and participate in joint action. The capacity to do this not only ensures acceptance by significant others but also reduces negative feelings of insecurity, anxiety and powerlessness.

From a sociological perspective what individuals try to do in their interactions with others is to construct and maintain an acceptable version of themselves (Weick, 1995). All of us are constantly involved in accounting for ourselves to others: describing what we have done or are about to do, explaining why, and shaping and transmitting our experience in a way that fits in with local conventions. To do this we have to find out what counts as acceptable in order that we can match our description of our practice and experience to it.

This accounting for the self is always negotiated because its success will depend on whether the listener(s) go along with the individual's version of events. In the longer term it also needs the other(s) to affirm his or her account. The individual needs to be woven into the stories of others and equally needs to reciprocate so that the group consistently maintains a socially negotiated framework for sense-making that meets the needs of the individual and the group. It is in these social interactions that the individual's identity is formed by the process of adjusting to the dominant discourse of those group(s) in the social environment who are influential and important for that individual (Bourdieu, 1977).

What has been described so far is often conceptualised as socialisation. A reason for being wary of this term is that it has the connotation of being a one-off process that occurs when an individual first joins an organisation, the assumption being that, once the person is socialised, these processes cease to operate. The constructionist view is that sense-making is a dynamic social process that is subject to continual revision and negotiation. Thus socialisation continues to be a factor in determining the behaviour of all members of the organisation, regardless of whether they are probationers or experienced staff. This concept therefore gives us a useful lens for examining the process of CPD.

We have said that the prevailing norms of the workplace shape the individual's identity and the social processes involved place a considerable pressure to conform. Individuals are left with three possible responses to the identity/position assigned to them through the local discourse:

1) Accepting and internalising it.
2) Complying with it but maintaining internal opposition.
3) Contesting and rejecting it (Burr, 1995).

The logic here, in terms of change, is that if established members of the group alter their practice they cannot adopt the first position (equivalent to absorption), nor the second. They will have to adopt the third position either through trying to modify the current view of what makes for acceptable practice (seek an accommodation with the local discourse) or by becoming more openly oppositional and uncompromising (revolution, seeking to overturn the local discourse and substitute a new one). There are clear personal and emotional risks inherent in this latter approach. For many it will be easier to adopt the second position (maintain internal opposition) and simply let the new learning atrophy.

Applying this idea to professional development, one way to consider a course is as a social context. In the inter-relationship between teachers and learners (for instance, where the learners regard the teacher as having prestige and credibility), the learners are more likely to want to give a good account of themselves as students and of the worth of their engagement in the course. Equally, particularly on a long course, their fellow learners will often have a strong influence on their conduct through establishing what it means to be part of this particular cohort. In this sense we can look at a course as establishing its own particular social setting and culture. However, in terms of determining what counts as good practice and worthwhile development for course members who are also employed, there is a more crucial type of social setting – each individual's workplace.

Schools as environments for social learning

This process of social learning is graphically illustrated in Kainan's (1994) study of a staffroom in a comprehensive school. She concludes (*ibid.* 157) that the staffroom is where the 'norms, premises and values' are developed that tend to bind all the teachers in the school:

> Teachers use it [the staffroom] and the interactions that take place within it to define situations. In the staffroom, the regular actors [the teachers] act simultaneously as actors and audience. Each of the teachers represents him/herself to his/her colleagues, and an interaction develops among the teachers, based on each teacher's interpretation of the situation.

Evans (1999), in her work on teacher motivation, points to very similar processes. According to her evidence the successful or unsuccessful socialisation of teachers into a school is linked to the match between their own professionality and the level of professionalism prevailing in that school. Here she quotes an experienced teacher commenting on the effect of having a new headteacher shortly before taking up a new post in another school (*ibid.*: 44):

> In my opinion, not only has the school not moved on, but we've actually moved backwards! All the 'extended professionals', are just going there's nobody in the school with any vision – nobody with any educational philosophy – and that's what really frightens me to death . . .

Because, they think that you just go in and you teach, therefore children will learn. They don't seem to realise what a curriculum really is.

Kainan's (1994) study also shows the pressure to conform being applied to established members of staff, not just newcomers. Established staff will already have a recognised professional persona amongst their colleagues. If one of them undergoes a programme of study that alters his or her perception and understanding of aspects of classroom practice, he or she will probably have to challenge this identity at some point. This will involve changing the way in which he or she accounts to colleagues for any resultant change in practice.

Isolation and autonomy

There is a consistent body of research that indicates schools provide poor environments for the professional development of teachers. School teaching is characterised by the isolation of teachers in their own classrooms with a consequent lack of opportunity for them to interact with their colleagues during the work of teaching, and this is compounded by the tradition of teacher autonomy. This has two effects. First, it means that in many ways the pupils are the teacher's most influential referent group and, secondly, it severely limits the basis for developing a strong technical culture of teaching through professional discussion and interaction amongst teachers.

One striking feature of teachers' accounts of their working lives is the crucial part that pupils, and their own perceptions from when they themselves were pupils, play in defining what it is to be 'a good teacher'. Jenny Nias (1988), in a study of successful primary teacher's attitudes to the job, showed the close link teachers felt between their personal and their classroom identity. The influence the class had on enabling them to maintain this identity is evident from Nias's statement (*ibid*. 204) that many of her respondents remarked that 'they hated "being a policemen"; the times "when you can't do any teaching because you spend all day keeping them down"; or "children who force you to act in ways you know have nothing to do with teaching" '.

Recent work by Weber and Mitchell (1996) showed how prevalent conventional images of teaching are amongst both pupils and student teachers. The implications of these findings are that the teacher's milieu for altering practice is particularly restrictive. The dominance of a strongly stereotyped and 'dated identity', determined by pupils who, because of their youth and position as observers rather than practitioners, have no basis for critical involvement in shaping and developing teaching practice, provides little room for a growth in professionalism.

The second effect was noted by Lortie (1975), who first drew attention to the relatively weak socialisation processes of professional induction prevalent in teaching. The opportunities for novices to observe, trial, discuss and develop technical aspects of teaching were few – he described induction as a largely 'sink-or-swim' affair (*ibid.*: 60). He contended that this led, in turn, to a lack of a shared technical culture that has limited the development of professionalism within education. After this initial phase the effects of teacher isolation and autonomy compound the problem.

Since many teachers still rarely observe each other teaching or participate in collaborative approaches to teaching, their opportunities for engaging in discussions about practice are often quite limited. This lack of opportunity for professional dialogue tends to breed a culture where practice is not something that is subject to debate and analysis.

There is a very clear instance of this from Huberman's (1993) intensive study of teachers' working lives in Switzerland. Huberman expressed surprise at the way in which the non-mastery of certain aspects of teaching was treated 'quite serenely' by teachers and how this situation could prevail for years without apparently causing any great heartache on their part (*ibid.*: 256). In a work context where the teacher received little or no feedback from other practitioners there was no social/professional mechanism to warrant improvement.

Additionally, where the teachers did try to address these issues their strategies often reflected an over-reliance on their personal resources:

> teachers in our sample rarely turn to in-service training in order to remedy non-mastery. They prefer procedures of remediation that are informal and individual – a swarm of private experiments. Reflection on pedagogical practice was not lacking in initial training or in continued education. But there was a tendency for these informal moments to end up with somewhat lax, disabused conclusions, sometimes leading to professional uneasiness or disengagement (*ibid.*).

Thus professional isolation set limits to these teachers' capacity for effective reflection. Even when they did experiment this was often poorly structured and led to limited and sometimes questionable solutions to issues of practice.

Adding to this rather doom-laden view is the final observation on the generally negative attitudes of teachers to change: 'and is it not institutional norms that dictate the conditions under which, with experience, teachers become more cautious, mistrustful toward changes and reforms and more fatalistic in terms of their degrees of freedom and means of action' (*ibid.*: 259).

Group and organisational effects

Having emphasised the isolating effects of teachers' working conditions, this does not mean there are no significant adult referents for teachers. One of the major influences on individual teacher satisfaction in Huberman's (1993) study is the establishment of professional acceptability within a small group of other teachers.

This finding is illuminated further in the work of Talbert and McLaughlin (1996), who conducted an investigation into influences on the professional standards of high-school teachers in the USA. They found that professional standards varied according to sector (private/public), district, school and subject department. However, the greatest influence on teachers' views of professionalism and the task of teaching comes through their immediate teacher community (i.e. the group of teachers with whom they felt most closely associated). Generally the subject department exerted the strongest influence on teacher attitudes. However, the analysis showed this was not due to the nature of the subject but rather to the particular department's culture – an indication that strong teacher communities do promote shared norms of practice – a finding that correlates with findings from school effectiveness studies in the UK (Sammons *et al.*, 1997).

Not only are there clear lines of influence to an immediate referent group but the effect of the school is also well documented within the extensive research on school effectiveness. The junior schools project, undertaken by Mortimore *et al.* for the ILEA (1988), focused on classroom practice, headteacher behaviours and the school norms present in effective schools.

This is one of a number of studies that point to the crucial role of the headteacher in influencing and establishing the school culture. In many schools in the UK, the head's views will carry considerable weight with individual members of staff. As a result they will be concerned to conform to his or her attitudes and beliefs about the characteristics of the 'good teacher' or will have to adopt an oppositional stance (Table 4.1).

From a slightly different angle, Louis and Smith (in Reyes, 1990) surveyed the literature on aspects of the quality of working life in education and other sectors that were associated with improved commitment. Of the seven factors they identify, five relate to social issues:

Table 4.1 Teacher/headteacher behaviours and school norms in effective junior schools

Classroom behaviour	Headteacher behaviour	School norms
Consistency of teacher practice, structured teaching sessions, intellectually challenging teaching. Work-centred talk, purposive and enthusiastic, good communication.	Involvement in curricular discussion. Delegation/sharing responsibility, knowledge of classrooms and pupils. Monitoring of pupil achievement. Promotes staff development. Open to parents.	Teacher participation and involvement in decision-making. High expectations of pupil achievement. Parental involvement.

Source: Adapted from Mortimore *et al.* (1988: 250–62).

1) Respect from relevant adults.
2) Participation in decision-making.
3) Frequent and stimulating professional interaction.
4) A high sense of efficacy.
5) Personal goal congruence with the organisation.

Rosenholtz (1989) links several of these school-level factors (with the addition of feedback on performance) to increased teacher certainty about what constitutes effective practice and hence to improved performance.

Aspiration and affiliation

Returning to our opening argument, it is important that teachers see the outcomes of any learning they undertake as legitimated by a group whose approval they respect and/or desire. Linda Evans' (1999) research points very clearly to the importance of this factor in her exploration of the concept of 'professionality', which she defines (*ibid.*: 38) as encompassing a teacher's

• professional ideology;
• job-related values; and
• vision.

People need a vision of what they may become that is motivating and that offers them an opportunity for growth that will also command respect and support amongst those colleagues whose opinions matter to them.

This could be quite disheartening because change for the better will almost certainly involve unpicking or challenging the prevailing view of practice in a particular school. There is plenty of evidence to show this may be done successfully by new headteachers, but where does this leave those with a less powerful role? Evidence in relation to the conversion of people from one value position to another shows that minorities are often surprisingly influential because they attract the attention of those in the majority and foster re-examination and argumentation about the status quo (Weick, 1995: 142). The Improving the Quality of Education for All project (Hopkins *et al.*, 1996) uses this effect in its development of the cadre structure as a means of promoting cultural change in support of inclusive education. Again what we are outlining here is the need for personal support and the backing of those involved in change within the workplace to enable both the exploration and adoption of new practice to occur.

To summarise the main points we have made so far: whilst we see the alteration in the perceptual frameworks of the individual as the key to developing and extending practice significantly, that this can only occur effectively within the social context of the workplace supported by professional dialogue. The individual's cognitive processes are driven and reinforced through social processes (Elkjaer, 1999).

We have to plan individual performance development with the whole school and its internal groupings in mind. The school has to be regarded as a critical part of the system for development because, without taking the social aspects of learning into account, the chances of implementation for the individual are materially reduced.

At a more strategic level one comes back to the contention of the school improvement movement that unless the isolationist tradition is broken, a more dynamic and open-ended culture that can support innovation and creativity cannot be developed.

Linking the learning processes

How can we think about putting these two aspects of learning (the reflective and the social) together? Schon (1983) makes some reference to this issue when he says we need to think about reflection as involving the three dimensions as shown in Figure 4.4. One way of tying the two together in rather more specific terms is by looking at the possible social contexts that could be offered to teachers. We might place the cognitive processes at centre-stage in our model and then 'surround' them by the social learning contexts that would be supportive of their development, as in Figure 4.5. The contexts shown in this figure on the left-hand side of the centre can have an important part to play in the individual's development, and they represent typical course structures. These are usually external to the school:

- Cohort networking where participants on the same programme or course can meet together. Fellow learners, as co-practitioners, can

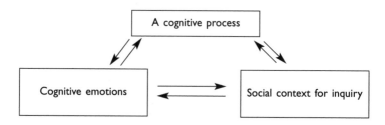

Figure 4.4 Reflection

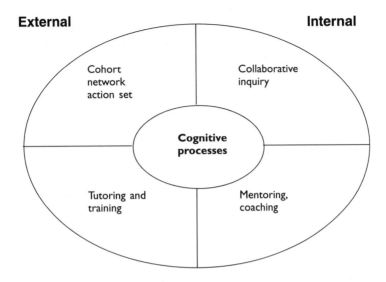

Figure 4.5 A structured model for sense-making

assist in providing validation for each other and a supportive social context for learning and experimenting with new ideas.
- Tutoring and training can also provide support and encouragement and a context for testing and developing ideas. Depending on the credibility of the tutors within the school context, they can also provide validation.

These two contexts can have an important part to play but without those on the right-hand side there will be no real extension into the workplace:

- Collaborative inquiry into practice in the school in some form is necessary so there is a supportive referent group for the individual whose members also have a stake in supporting the new practice and can support each other in solving the problems of implementation.
- Mentoring/coaching and backing provided by someone with credibility and power within the school will also be crucial in providing validation and both practical and socio-political support.

Improvement and development of practice must have a strong locus in work-based learning and this, in turn, has significant implications for the way in which professional development opportunities are both structured and supported. It implies the provision of professional development needs to become an essential function of all schools and that schools will also need the means to connect to the wider knowledge base through partnerships and structures that will support networking and mixed modes of provision of professional development opportunities.

Conclusions

To summarise the outcomes of this discussion, there seem to be five main features of changing practice that need to be taken into account in planning for improved performance:

1) First, and most importantly, practice has to be seen as a core element of the learning process if we are serious about improving performance. Neglect of this as part of the planned structure for learning means the outcomes of any intervention are generally likely to be of limited success.

2) Without the acquisition of new ideas, understandings and experiences to provide a tool kit for interrogating performance, significant and important gains in practice are unlikely to occur.

3) The involvement of significant others in the workplace in the learning process is critical to the success of individuals.

4) To embed significant change in practice the learner needs to be able to tap into sources of personal support at a social, emotional and technical level.

5) Finally, professional dialogue is crucial to the cognitive processes underlying professional change as a setting for requiring and enabling the various key cognitive operations to take place.

Our next task is to look at current approaches to work-based learning to see how they match up to our learning model for improving professional performance.

5

Work-based learning

Introduction

In Chapter 4 we argued there were two fundamental learning processes (the reflective and the social) that need to be engaged in order to improve performance. These two processes are constantly in operation in the workplace but without some structuring their content and the quality of their outcomes will be variable. We have also indicated that schools are a relatively impoverished setting for adult learning, and both custom and working conditions do not make it easy for individual teachers to improve their practice. The habit of providing professional development off-site and ignoring the school as a learning environment for adults compounds these problems. How, then, should schools shape these processes to support improvement in performance?

This chapter looks at the main forms of structured intervention aimed at improving performance that are used in school settings, and it sets out to gauge their strengths and weaknesses. The issues this examination raises point to a number of dilemmas that employers, school managers and their staff need to consider in implementing the drive to improvement.

Structuring work-based learning

Most staff development initiatives in the field of education have been work focused. They have depended on instruction in the form of taught or distance-learning courses, the content of which is of relevance to the work of participants. However, work-focused learning is not the same as work-based learning (WBL), which we are defining as taking place in the course of practice in the person's normal work context. Our argument, like that of others in the field (Joyce *et al.*, 1999), is not that all learning relevant to practice has to be work based but rather that without its inclusion as a substantive part of the planned learning programme effects on performance will be slight. Many in-service education and training (INSET) initiatives have disappeared without trace (Bradley *et al.*, 1994) because new skills and understandings are not transferred to the school setting. Structured WBL is essential to bridging this transfer gap.

Following from the key features of provision we put forward in Chapter 4, the key elements in programmes designed to enhance performance can be distilled into four sets of characteristics:

1) *Reflection on practice* The place given to self-evaluation of performance in terms of both identifying learning needs and assessing whether practice has changed for the better as a result of the learning process; access to feedback on performance.
2) *Experiential learning* The structured opportunities for experimenting with practice as a basis for learning in the work situation available to the learner.
3) *Cognitive development* The tools and opportunities available to enable learners to think about their experience in ways that will enhance their understanding and help to create a rich and meaningful framework to support skilled practice.
4) *Social learning processes* The social circumstances that will support cognitive development and the adoption of new practice on the part of the individual; socially validated rewards for engagement.

How can these four elements be used to achieve learning for improvement within any given programme or approach to staff development?

Traditionally in the UK, most planned continuing professional development (CPD) for teachers has consisted of short courses provided by either local authority or other trainers and, more occasionally, longer courses, usually associated with higher education awards. Most short courses try to do something about the third element, cognitive development, in terms of influencing attitudes and assumptions through the provision of information and the advocacy of a particular 'piece' of practice, together with opportunities (through the use of workshops) to develop learners' skills. The fourth element, social processes, is treated fairly superficially through the appeal to expert authority and legitimation; and the fleeting social opportunities to interact with other course members, the first and second elements, which focus on practice and the use of experience, are usually noticeable by their absence.

Longer courses often place more emphasis on particular aspects of cognitive development, but this may have only weak links with experience in terms of practice in the workplace. Practical activity, as with the short courses, may still be largely confined to using skills during workshops consisting of simulations and role plays. Stronger social processes may also be built in through the tutor (mentor) role and through the cohort group, where the longer timescale allows for the development of closer and more professionally influential relationships. Increasingly such courses have tried (through the assessment process) to involve candidates in work-based projects with some focusing on criteria that have a direct connection with performance, although this is still an exception.

These designs need to be substantially reviewed if the supposed target of CPD, the enhancement of performance of the individual, is to be achieved. We have argued that the effective enhancement and support of WBL are essential to this process. There are a number of other common criticisms of current provision WBL can also help to address:

- The frequent complaint by many teachers that staff development interventions are irrelevant because they do not help them to achieve greater success in the classroom. Structured WBL offers the possibility of ensuring that professional development focuses constructively on teachers' work.
- The need for the learning of the individual to be validated and supported in the workplace. WBL allows for the negotiation and matching of individual and organisational needs and, therefore, offers a greater likelihood of incorporation into the social processes of the school.
- One of the weaknesses of the profession is seen by a number of commentators as the general lack of a developed scientific and procedural knowledge about teaching, both on the part of individuals and the profession as a whole. WBL could be structured to address this deficiency through an emphasis on processes of professional inquiry.

Of course all this is not new and there are a number of WBL schemes already in place that focus on influencing performance. We shall turn now to analysing three common methods of performance enhancement that entail structuring of WBL in one form or another.

Existing approaches to WBL

Approaches to WBL can be thought of as falling under a number of broad headings that encompass most current approaches to staff development. As with any typology this tends to put an overemphasis on difference whereas, as we show in the following discussion, approaches are frequently mixed rather than purely of one type or another. These categories are:

- managerial
- craft/professional
- organisational development.

We shall look at each of these in terms of a brief description, the assumptions underpinning the approach, roles and responsibilities, the preferred mode of assessment, mode of learning, rewards and a discussion of strengths and weaknesses.

It can be argued that the managerial approach is not properly focused on staff development. However, in line with our contention that changes in performance are the result of learning, it legitimately falls within the WBL category for the purposes of analysis.

Managerial methodologies

Managerial methodologies are based on a technical-rational approach to performance and are dependent upon the traditional relationship within industry and commerce of the line manager to the managed. In this sense they have grown out of a relationship of supervision and a culture where 'Managers are paid to get results and developing their staff contributes to achieving that goal' (Hamilton, 1993: 2). The underlying assumption here is that, if the individuals who make up the workforce do the 'right things right', the performance of the whole organisation will be enhanced. The major concern is to enhance quality and dependability and cut wastage and costs (Flood, 1998).

The approach is initiated from the top down since the framework for identifying and meeting development needs is usually set by the organisation's senior management, although this may be 'softened' by consultation and negotiation with the workers. The standard industrial procedure for performance management (appraisal plus staff development) is often described in the accompanying literature as a way of matching and meeting individual and organisational needs.

Ideally this approach makes learning requirements very explicit and clear through the use of detailed job descriptions and/or competence standards that serve as the basis for evaluating the learner's current performance. From this evaluation targets for development are agreed and the list of competences serves as a basis for planning the experiences that will be required to ensure the learner can develop skills and behaviours that are currently judged to be absent or in need of refining. Whether development opportunities are arranged in the workplace or outside it, there is an assumption they will lead to a measurable improvement of performance. The salient features of the approach are as follows:

- The job requirements and underlying competences (performance measures) are clearly defined and shared.
- The line manager and the employee look at how well the employee's performance matches up to the standards required.
- Gaps in the employee's competence (skills and knowledge) are identified through this process.
- These 'gaps' form the basis for agreeing the individual's targets for development.
- The targets are put into action within an agreed timescale.
- The employee's performance is then measured against the standard and, hopefully, the feedback shows there has been improvement.

Although the methodology can obviously allow for the recognition and validation of good practice, the assumptions behind it are largely remedial since the spur to action is the failure of the employee's performance to reach a desired standard. Obviously this need not be a critical situation in that the person may have just taken on the job or the job may have been altered to include new requirements for competence. In these cases there is clearly the possibility for growth. Additionally, development could be focused on next steps for the employee in furthering his or her career.

The role of the line manager is to ensure that individuals' targets for performance and development needs in relation to the organisation's requirements are identified and agreed and that there is a 'contract' with each employee to secure improvement. It is also the manager's responsibility to ensure that the employee is given an opportunity to improve by providing access to relevant experience as required. Employees on their part undertake to meet the targets for improvement on this basis.

Assessment of the success or otherwise of the steps taken to enhance the employee's development is based on performance indicators derived from the job description or the standard. The standard serves as a template for learning as well as a basis for assessment.

The assessor is normally the line manager. The learner is thus provided with feedback on performance.

In those cases where individual progress is linked to the acquisition of vocational qualifications the learner makes a formal claim to have achieved the performance targets backed either by paper evidence or the observation of performance by an internal assessor. The judgement of the internal assessor is then subject to external verification by an accrediting body.

This approach is usually linked, directly or indirectly, to a structured reward system that may deploy a variety of incentives for the recognition of success. There is usually an emphasis on extrinsic rewards as the basis for motivation:

- *Economic* Performance-related pay, one-off payments, bonuses, share deals, etc.
- *Career* The employee is considered as ready to move to the next step on a clear career ladder within the organisation. Fast tracking through the career structure may be offered for people who are considered to show outstanding potential for development.
- *Recognition* Accreditation of learning through formal qualifications. These may also act as gateways to the career structure (e.g. the need to pass the sergeant's examination before being considered for a sergeant's post in the police force). Publication and celebration – employee of the year, photo in the newsletter, etc., particular privileges and perks.

The link between the appraisal and development procedure and the reward system may be either direct or indirect. For instance, qualifications usually have an immediate and direct link with the appraisal process whereas the determination of monetary awards may either be incorporated as part of the appraisal process or be implemented through a separate procedure.

This gives the basic outline of the approach that, on the face of it, is best suited to processes of absorption on the part of both the organisation and the individual:

1) as a way of structuring the learning of relatively new employees; or
2) supporting refinements in practice that involve relatively minor changes in knowledge and skills for more established staff.

However, this is a somewhat naïve assumption because of the underlying power structure. The system may obviously be used on the part of the management group as a means for changing the culture of the organisation (i.e. to foster accommodation or even revolution in terms of practical learning because the managers have substantial control over the terms that define desired practice). One of the appeals of human resources management (HRM) to senior managers is the claim that it serves as a strategic instrument for bringing about substantive cultural change (Stewart and McGoldrick, 1996: 10; Armstrong and Baron, 1998: 8).

In this regard many organisations are now moving away from straightforward job descriptions and related standards to targets based on the values and core competences of the organisation. For instance, in British Telecom five core capabilities are used in the appraisal process, and these apply to all members of staff regardless of their particular job or grading:

1) seizing opportunities;
2) delighting customers;
3) releasing potential;
4) setting direction; and
5) working together.

Each of these are then typified by a series of defined behaviours.

This trend makes the link between individual and organisational targets more direct and flexible and ties in with an increasing emphasis on the management of values as the key managerial art (Cray and Mallory, 1998; Griseri, 1998; Parker, 1998). It also means that clear links are established between the employees' behaviours and key targets for the organisation whatever the person's particular remit may be.

Strengths and weaknesses

In terms of learning the managerial approach has a major strength that touches on both the cognitive and the social aspects of development. Learners are very clear about what is expected of them. The paperwork and discussions with their managers enable them to make sense of their experience and to understand the prevailing discourse within the organisation with regard to their work roles. The learners know what their story ought to be and how they should construct their work identities. They have a framework to guide their performance in the 'right' direction. This is strengthened by the 'respect' shown to them through the time given by a significant other to personal discussion and negotiation.

The specification of expectations, whether in the form of descriptions of employees' remits or a defined standard or set of capabilities, allows them to direct their own learning towards achieving the targets they have been set in line with a number of aspects of current motivational theory (Cooper and Locke, 2000). Through a process of self-evaluation the employees can determine for themselves the next steps they need to take to improve their performance. In this sense the process can foster independent learning and improved self-confidence. The employee also receives feedback on performance that again serves both as a form of personal validation, if the feedback is positive, and as an opportunity further to refine and clarify expectations.

The methodology provides a transparent system that makes expectations very clear and should, therefore, be supportive of equal opportunities. Nepotism, sponsorship and other forms of prejudicial practice should be more difficult to sustain. The managerial approach is also accessible since it ensures a regular review for each member of the organisation. In that sense it can be seen as providing an entitlement to development opportunities for all staff.

This methodology is ostensibly efficient because it ensures the proper targeting of resources and effort through the clear identification of development needs and the evaluation of outcomes on the basis of measurable performance. This is not simply an economic gain for the organisation; it should also defend employees from being frustrated and disappointed by a lack of appropriate provision and/or being unfairly treated as a result of poor performance which they have had no opportunity to improve.

On the other hand, the methodology is inclined to lead to a very individualistic approach to development. This arguably leads to two weaknesses. First, whilst individuals may be making the links to common goals for the organisation, their targets and learning experiences are individually planned, thus weakening the link to the collective. Further, the achievement of targets is centred on individual gain. Deming (1982) was scathing in his criticism of the system on this account, and feedback from a recent survey of performance management arrangements also points to some of the possible pitfalls:

> People have their objectives on a piece of paper and they know their money is based on these objectives. And, as a result of that, they compromise other areas in terms of the whole picture to meet these objectives, because they are not actually measured on whether they have messed someone else up (Quoted in Armstrong and Baron, 1998: 172).

In this sense the methodology can cut across a commitment to a team approach to organisational learning and development.

There are trenchant critics of the drive to transparency through the use of standards who claim, not without a hint of snobbery, that the establishment of clear outcomes for performance limits learning to a narrow behaviourist range. This, it is argued, is unsuitable for workers in the professional field where flexible responses to problematic situations rather than the reliable repetition of known behaviours are the desired outcome of development (Barnett, 1994).

More fundamentally there is a potential clash with the premises of professional accountability, which emphasise the intrinsic moral responsibility of professionals continually to develop their expertise in the interests of their clients and the professional community (Eraut, 1994). As a result of these duties professionals claim a right to autonomy and freedom of action that sits uneasily with the notion of line management and the detailed specification of practice.

Linked to this is the further criticism that the system curbs creativity and learning on the part of both individuals and the organisation because it is based on norms of past practice and discourages experimentation and risk-taking. Politically, too, it can be seen as suppressing the underlying pluralism of the organisation, although it is often argued to be a means of furthering a two-way system of communication (Winstanley and Stuart-Smith, 1996).

Since the approach is about ensuring conformity to already agreed parameters this may raise difficulties with experienced staff who may well feel offended and belittled by the process as they believe they already fulfil their role effectively. Agreeing targets that command the commitment of the employee can be quite difficult under these circumstances.

As the managerial approach is informed by a set of motivational models (Drucker, 1954) rather than theories of learning, the overall place and design of opportunities for staff development do leave something to be desired. The major contribution of the approach lies in the developmental use of standards as a means for employees to structure their own learning in the workplace where it has rather more impact on the social learning process than it does on the cognitive cycle. The system of negotiation and agreement around an explicit set of norms provides the employee with a degree of security about what is required. It also ensures a sharing of the discourse of management within the organisation and in that it is helpful in enabling employees to socialise themselves into the officially legitimated framework.

As we have defined it theoretically, the managerial approach should match the desirable elements in structured WBL as shown in Table 5.1. Its major weaknesses lie in the lack of any real model for

Table 5.1   The managerial model and the four elements of WBL

Reflection on practice	• Starting with a supported reflective and evaluative process focusing on outcomes of performance in the workplace. • Using an evaluative process to assess the learner's achievement in terms of the agreed targets for practice. • Providing feedback on performance to the learner.
Experiential learning	(*Variable depending on the organisation.*)
Cognitive development	• Making the expectations of the learner clear and specific. Providing opportunities for the discussion of performance.
Social processes	• Securing the commitment of the learner to a course of action. • Using social processes to secure attention and to transmit value. • Introducing the learner to the desired social norms and the official discourse of the organisation. • Validating change through a powerful set of significant others by giving the learner a mandate and support from the managers.

learning other than the rationalist assumption that if learners know exactly what is required of them they can set about achieving it, and the narrowness of provision for cognitive development. Obviously the latter might be improved through the staff development opportunities offered to the individual by the organisation.

Craft/professional methodologies

The set second of methodologies (craft/professional) are based upon the idea that someone new to a trade or profession learns best by working alongside an experienced practitioner who can act as a role model, guide and support. This is a classic model for learning that predates schooling, so it has certainly stood the test of time (Lave and Wenger, 1991). The assumptions upon which it is based contrast quite sharply with the technical-rational model that underpins managerial approaches.

The master and pupil roles are as unequal as those of line manager and employee but ideally the relationship is based on personal respect for the superior professional merit of the master rather than on a contractual/bureaucratic connection. It is also the responsibility and duty of the mentor or master to meet the needs of the learner in acquiring mastery of their trade. Originally the learner either paid the master or offered his services to him free of charge as a return for this introduction to the craft.

Under the tutelage of the master, the apprentice learnt by:

- watching how the master performed;
- trialling increasingly complex elements of practice whilst receiving feedback on performance (coaching);
- being sponsored within the trade by the master (given entry to the relevant networks like the guild, etc.); and
- finally, producing a piece of work that, if judged by other masters to be of sufficient quality, entitled him to formal recognition as a master in his own right.

In this model there is no formal point at which there is an evaluation of need. The mentor engages in continuous formative assessment and guidance but not in the summative assessment of performance. An outline of mentoring in teacher education given by Anderson and Shannon (1995: 32) shows that the model has changed very little over the years:

- teach
- sponsor
- encourage
- counsel
- befriend.

Mentoring was not traditionally part of the induction of new teachers in the UK although it has gained ground in recent years both as a formal element in initial teacher education in England and Wales and during the probationary period following qualification across the UK (MacIntyre, 1997).

Mentoring is also increasingly being used at later stages in teachers' careers where there is a change in responsibility, such as entry to middle and whole-school management (Smith and West-Burnham, 1993; Southworth, 1995). Mentoring links between established school leaders and senior managers from industry are established as an integral part of the Leadership Programme for Serving Headteachers (LPSH).

Rewards in the craft/professional model are less clearly structured than in the managerial model and, traditionally, rest on the basic assumption that individuals' main allegiance is to their profession rather than to the organisation they happen to work in. Thus:

- *Economic* In so far as gaining a licence to practise gives entry into the trade/profession.
- *Career* There are often specialisations within the craft or profession that are seen as requiring a further period of formal and work-based learning. This may be linked to professional qualifications and/or the recognition of merit of output may provide a basis for promotion (e.g. consultants in medicine, the status of reader or professor in higher education).
- *Recognition* The professional network provides a structure for connoisseurship in relation to practice, a basis for the acquisition of a reputation for excellence within the trade which, in turn, can lead to financial rewards; certain professional bodies will invite or offer membership on this basis; and, at an informal level, people acquire reputations within the field, becoming revered voices in the trade/profession.

Assessment within this system is based on formal recognition by senior colleagues that the person has satisfactorily fulfilled the terms of the practicum. This will also be linked in several of the professions to formal examination, either for a qualification or for membership of recognised professional groupings (for example, Member of the Institute of Chemical Engineers). Prestigious professional associations may only allow membership on the basis of the recognition of outstanding merit (for example, Fellow of the Royal Society).

Strengths and weaknesses

The major strength of the approach lies in the model of learning that underpins it, which allows for the effective combination of both cognitive and social learning elements. Mentoring provides the means for a very close match to the development of practice in context. The individuality of the relationship potentially allows experience to be very precisely tailored to the learner's particular needs. The discussion involved develops frameworks of meaning and deals with role and identity issues at a personal and individual level within a confidential and 'safe' relationship.

The closeness and supportive nature of the relationship (where it works well) provide a strong social basis for learning and can command great loyalty on the part of the learner to the practice. There is the possibility of raising professional expectations with a push towards excellence that goes beyond contentment with basic competence. The model also allows for transmission of tacit and detailed craft knowledge through the system of demonstration and direct coaching, which would be impossible to write into competence statements or to communicate easily in the context of a taught course.

Sponsorship and bridging activities on the part of the mentor into relevant networks give the learner an entry into the social system that prevails within the profession. Both through the mentor and the access to other practitioners the new entrant learns the dominant discourse and value system of the profession.

Providing the mentor is good at the job and can devote sufficient time to it, the approach is very efficient in supporting the development of the learner. However, because mentoring carries quite a high cost it can be divisive (for instance, some organisations only use mentoring for their 'high flyers').

With its origins in contexts where the practitioner was usually self-employed, the methodology fosters a basic pluralism because of its recognition of loyalty to the profession as well as to the organisation in which the learner works. This can have the advantage of strengthening the technical culture within the organisation and preserving a channel for the importation of new ideas.

For instance, within education it does offer a structure for developing a stronger technical culture of teaching. However, because the current technical culture of teaching is relatively weak (Hargreaves, 1996), moving to this system too quickly runs the risk of perpetuating indifferent practice (Hagger, 1997). This means there is a need to invest quite heavily in the quality of mentors. Current attempts in the UK to establish the status of Advanced Skills, Expert or Chartered Teacher could be seen as an attempt to achieve this, where these are linked to posts that require the incumbent to act as a tutor/mentor to others in the school.

However, there are a number of clear disadvantages to the craft/professional approach. Mentoring is not traditionally based on an open or transparent revelation of expectations. In fact, its origins lie in preserving trade secrets. It is therefore open to operating in ways that are prejudicial and exclusionary to particular individuals or groups. Further, the closeness of the relationship between the mentor and the learner runs the danger of fostering dependency and cliqueism in some circumstances. Learners are not encouraged to be critical of their mentors and they may become attached, through personal loyalty, to a poor model of practice.

In terms of conservatism and conformity, mentoring can be subject to much the same criticisms as the standards used in the managerial approach. Mentoring is essentially about the 'experienced' training the 'inexperienced'. As a result it has an in-built conservatism. The learner is being inducted into an existing culture that may have been handed down from mentor to learner for several generations.

In fact one of the major criticisms of professional training is that it is too self-referential. The traditional definitions and structure of professionalism are seen to offer little encouragement to be accountable to those outside the profession. A tendency to connoisseurship may distract proper attention to outcomes for clients leading to a definition of practice that is dominated by the interests of the profession. The argument here is that professionals may become so enwrapped in impressing other practitioners or adopting the practice which is professionally 'fashionable' that they are no longer concentrating on their clients' best interests. An example of this within education was the view of those who railed against the predominance of 'trendy' notions of child-centredness in the 1980s which, they saw, as leading to the neglect of basic skills teaching in schools.

To summarise the main features of the craft/professional model, it should match with our criteria for WBL as shown in Table 5.2. The major weakness of the approach is its lack of connection to the collective or work organisation as such. The problems this may cause can be particularly acute in multi-professional work contexts.

Organisational development methodologies

These approaches have their origin in the work of social psychologists and its further development in the hands of management

Table 5.2 The craft model and the four elements of WBL

Reflection on practice	• Focusing on performance.
	• Ensuring conformity to a professionally defined standard that is embedded in practice.
Experiential learning	• Modelling and coaching in relation to practice.
Cognitive development	• Introducing and developing the commonly held frameworks of reference for the profession as tools for the learner through dialogue with the mentor.
	• Enabling a professional dialogue on improving practice to take place with an informed focus on work behaviour.
Social processes	• Securing social acceptance and the establishment of professional identity through sponsorship and networking.
	• Providing validation for learning through the attention of a respected professional.

consultants. The entry into education has largely been through the agency of the school improvement movement that adopted many of the assumptions and processes of organisational development (OD) specialists (Schein, 1980).

The various models are based on the notion of the collective or team as the best medium for learning. As a consequence individual learning and performance are seen as being enhanced through participating in a collegial process of learning where everyone in the organisation works together to improve organisational outcomes. In this sense it is the mirror opposite of what we termed the managerial approach where the development of the individual is seen as ensuring the development of the organisation. Here the development of the organisation is seen as serving the needs of the individual.

The OD approach is based on Maslow's theory of motivation (1954), where the organisation is seen as allowing its members to achieve self-actualisation through their membership and to realise intrinsic personal goals for self-fulfilment. It also draws on the work of Lewin and his model of action research (1952) as the key to organisational learning and development. The key features of this model in terms of relationships are therefore:

- collegiality
- colleagueship
- a democratic sharing of responsibility
- joint endeavour for the common good
- leadership that is shared.

The organisational development model also assumes that the school has an organic and unpredictable relationship with its environment. Because this is constantly changing schools have to learn continuously to adjust their practice to achieve their goals.

Philosophically these ideas have a great deal of appeal to the teaching profession and they underpin the thinking of many of those in the school improvement movement (Fullan, 1991; Hargreaves and Hopkins, 1991; Stoll and Fink, 1996). The approach also has strong links to some of the basic philosophy of total quality management (TQM) (particularly Deming's ideas) and the currently popular notion of the learning organisation (Senge, 1996).

In the UK this approach to school improvement was promoted through the work of Lawrence Stenhouse (1975) in relation to action research. He saw the weakness of the research and diffusion model used in the UK by the Schools Council in the early 1960s as due to a failure to come to grips with the specifics of classroom practice and the social realities of the school. The solution was to assign greater responsibility and control over the development process to teachers.

Stenhouse believed that teachers had to surrender some professional autonomy. They had to be accountable for delivering generally agreed goals for education. This was to be achieved through participation in collaborative inquiry and research in order to find methodologies that led to real gains in achievement for pupils in their schools. Teachers needed to be committed to continuous school improvement and actively engage in bringing this about as a collective endeavour.

Within this paradigm there are a variety of positions (Figure 5.1). These range from that of Joyce *et al.* (1999) and Barber and Sebba's (1999) good practice model, where the role of school staff is collectively to engage in active diagnosis of learning and teaching processes in order to identify accurately the problems that need addressing. Once this is done they should select from a range of evidence-based packages of good practice that best fits with their preferred solution to the issue. Having made their selection they 'research' how to embed the new approach into their own practice and setting through a combination of staff development experiences: instruction, demonstration and co-coaching. At the other end of the spectrum is the freely floating action research model where teachers collectively or individually research their practice as the basis for improvement.

The commonest manifestation of the OD model is the school development planning process that became part of official government policy in the UK through the Education Reform Act 1988. As originally formulated by the Organisation for Economic Co-operation and Development (OECD), this was seen as the vehicle whereby the school, through self-evaluation, identified areas for improvement and then collectively decided on a methodology, adopted this and tested it by evaluating the results (Hargreaves and Hopkins, 1989; Holly and Southworth, 1989).

It follows, from its origins, that the rewards to the individual through the successful adoption of the OD strategy are largely intrinsic:

- *Intrinsic/social* A greater sense of efficacy and involvement. Increased self-confidence and pleasure in doing the job well.
- *Recognition* Some personal recognition in that good schools become beacons for others.
- *Career* Possible advantages in terms of other schools being eager to appoint someone from a school that commands professional respect. Improved qualifications where the school enters into agreement with a higher education institute to support the staff in undertaking action research (Ainscow *et al.*, 1994).

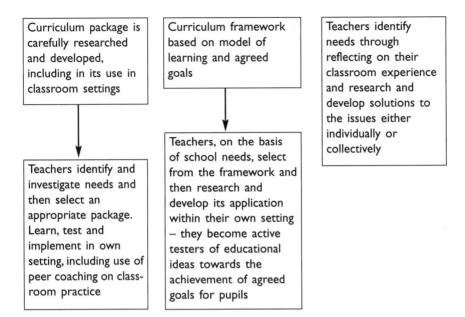

Figure 5.1 Variations on the community of inquiry/learning organisation model

Assessment of performance in relation to this model is predominantly collective in that it is the school's performance that is measured in terms of moving up the league tables and through improving its reputation both within the education service and the local (or wider) community.

Strengths and weaknesses

The strengths of the organisational development model lie in the potential it has for developing a culture of improvement through the sharing of discourse about teaching and learning, together with the availability of the social and emotional support that would enable individuals to experiment and incorporate new practices into their repertoire. This can lead to the creation of an exciting and innovative environment that encourages creative approaches and solutions in responding to the educational needs of children, young people and adults. The collective focus is also more likely to lead to the examination of processes that are often the key to improving performance and may not be as easily noticed/attended to using an individualistic approach to performance enhancement.

It is can also be seen as compatible with professional standards of accountability in that it ostensibly calls on a moral duty for providing the best possible service to clients as a basis for enhancing performance. In that sense the approach is far more acceptable to educationalists than the managerial model.

The appeal to evidence-based and research-based improvement provides for the tailoring of developments to particular contexts and allows room for experimentation and variation in approaches to practice. At least at the level of rhetoric, it could allow for creative responses to the need for change on the part of both individuals and schools as well as serving as a means for developing the technical culture of teaching through a structured approach to professional learning in the reality of schools and classrooms.

Lastly, it could be argued that the OD approach models the kind of relationships and approach to learning that is increasingly advocated for pupils and hence helps to make the school a place where models of teacher learning and involvement are compatible with the goals and system of student learning. The underlying principles should also allow for the development of a more team-based and democratic institution that would match better with the educational needs of students (Apple and Beane, 1998).

However, as with many of the issues in this field, the discourse of school improvement and development has been colonised and subverted to other ends. School development planning, rather than being a vehicle for schools to develop their own solutions to practice, has become an instrument for centralised control. Development plans for most schools are largely about compliance with centrally determined priorities and merely indicate how they will operationalise these directives. Essentially this use of the plans counters the learning advantages that were originally used to justify their introduction (Hargreaves and Hopkins, 1989).

There are some very clear limitations as well. Perhaps the most fundamental of these is that the approach is arguably unrealistic because both the traditions of teacher employment and the realities of current working conditions make the kind of collaboration and supportive framework that is envisaged almost impossible to implement. The change in attitudes and practices needed to underpin this approach requires significant alterations in the way schools are organised, the work of teachers is structured and teacher development is resourced and delivered.

Another criticism of this approach rests on the drawback of relying on a model that is largely school based. It could carry the danger of recycling poor practice so there needs to be a connection with a wider range of experience and the development of a strong technical culture to counteract this. Equally there is the danger of breeding a cosy collegiality where allegiance to the ethic that teacher satisfaction necessarily leads to good provision for children can all too easily be used to disguise sloppy performance.

There is also no mechanism – other than the goodwill and support of colleagues – for working directly on the issue of incompetence or generally responding in any systematic way to individual needs so that some teachers may respond much better to the process than others (Evans, 1999). The lack of clarity about what is required and the process of debate and exploration can be off-putting for those who learn better in a more structured environment.

In terms of our definition of WBL, the organisational development model should match our four elements as shown in Table 5.3.

Table 5.3 The OD model and the four elements

Reflection on practice	• With its concentration on improving learning outcomes, it does impinge on the self-evaluation of the performance and practice of teachers.
Experiential learning	• The action research model provides a practicable basis for fostering professional learning from experience.
Cognitive development	• Provides a context for reflection on practice and collaborative inquiry in relation to work experience. • Cognitively the engagement in dialogue and debate offers the potential for effective development.
Social processes	• Through collegial processes has the potential to provide a powerful social support for change and development based on professional dialogue. • Development planning does offer possibilities of achieving cultural congruity and validation for learning.

Implications for schools

We have mapped out some of the alternatives available for supporting improvement of performance. However, the central issue remains that of what will best support teacher learning. It seems to us that, with the introduction of contractual CPD and extrinsic rewards for teaching performance and the reintroduction of staff development and review (appraisal), employers and school managers have to think very carefully about exactly how they are going to work with their staff to enhance performance. Clearly there are a number of different underlying assumptions and attitudes involved in implementing these measures.

Even within the structure of the new framework school managers, governors and staffs have some choices to make about how to approach the issue of performance enhancement in their own schools. In making these decisions it is important to pay careful consideration to the various tensions that have been highlighted in the discussion in order to be clear about your rationale for the kind of practice that will be developed in your own context.

The tension between professional and managerial models of accountability.

How can you reconcile the traditions of professionality with new models of accountability? Have you thought through your position in relation to this issue and as to what principles and model of professionalism you are going to adopt in relation to your school's approach?

The tension between conformity and diversity, compliance and creativity?

Behind the use of some performance management techniques lies a mechanism for trying to ensure individuals conform to the culture of the school: one school, one vision, one staff, one community. How desirable is this? How do you balance valuing diversity and the creative tensions of difference with the increased drive and direction that come from a common commitment? How do you meet the need for reliably competent performance with the need for innovation, experimentation and risk-taking?

The tension between community and individualism?

Should you foster competition and reward individual achievement or is this counterproductive in terms of improving the overall performance of your school? How do you manage both fairness to individuals and to teams? How do you make a balance between developing a learning community and supporting individual learning needs?

Another obvious question that needs to be asked is: what are the performance issues in your school? Is there a general need to enhance/develop a culture of improvement, are your processes of induction weak, do you have some very competent practitioners who need re-energising and enthusing, do you have some teachers whose current performance is unsatisfactory? It may well be that the answer is 'yes' to all these, in which case you need to consider whether your approach is going to be flexible enough to meet all your needs.

Conclusion

As we can see from the discussion there are a range of issues to be addressed by managers in schools and other organisations as they establish and develop approaches to enhance the practice of individual members of staff in order to improve overall performance. Although in this chapter we have tried to delineate three contrasting models of WBL that are focused on improving practice, in many organisations where these systems are used they do not exist in a 'pure' form but are combined one with another. The most common of these combinations is a mixture of the managerial and the OD model best exemplified in forms of TQM and institutional standards such as Investors in People. Managerial and craft approaches are combined in schools in the UK during the induction period for newly qualified teachers where standards are used as a basis for assessing and providing feedback on performance together with mentoring. Another variant is to ally WBL with a more traditional training input. This has been a relatively common combination sponsored as part of the school improvement movement where an OD strategy is used together with a training/consultative input from higher education (Hopkins *et al.*, 1996; Stoll and Fink, 1996). Finally many organisations seek to modify the managerial approach through the use of a 'soft' strategy that stresses the self-evaluative and reflective elements of the process as against the supervisory relationship of the 'hard' version.

In order to illustrate further some of the issues we have outlined in this and the previous chapter we want to look in more detail at the lessons that have emerged from the implementation of a particular WBL scheme that employs elements of all three approaches: (managerial, craft and organisational development) in order to achieve improved performance.

We will be examining the implementation of the Scottish Qualification for Headship with a particular focus on:

- the structural implications of introducing WBL;
- the impact on individuals of the various elements of WBL; and
- the issues around the assessment of performance.

6

Building capability for work-based learning

Introduction

In Chapter 5 we outlined three models of work-based learning (WBL), each of which is founded on a different set of assumptions about improving personal and organisational effectiveness. We now want to explore some of the issues raised in WBL at a more practical level by looking at the experience of introducing the Scottish Qualification for Headship (SQH). The SQH is a programme of staff development designed to enhance the individual's performance and to contribute to the school's ongoing development. The introduction of the SQH has raised a number of issues particularly around the question of building capability at school level, in local authorities and amongst other providers. We will draw on the experience of establishing the programme to examine some of these issues.

The SQH combines a number of features drawn from all three models examined in the last chapter since it:

- uses a standard that defines the functions, values and abilities required for school leadership (managerial model);
- involves assessment of performance against the standard by both the learner and others (managerial model);
- requires learners to work with others to undertake projects in school to further the school's development priorities (organisational development model);
- uses mentoring with each learner having a more experienced manager acting as his or her critical friend and supporter in undertaking the school projects (craft/professional model); and
- uses an action research paradigm in that learners are required to plan, take action and review what has been learned and achieved (organisational development model).

In planning and continuing to develop the programme we have had to grapple with many of the challenges posed in Chapter 5. We have experienced the difficulties of trying to find a balance between the individual participant's needs and rights and the needs of the whole-school community, between the demands of development and accountability, between promoting current orthodoxies of good practice and the need to encourage creativity and innovation. The SQH programme also needed to address the aspirations of different stakeholders, particularly local authorities, schools and universities in ways that would support individual participants. In this chapter we shall explore some of these tensions by examining some of the decisions we came to in the process of building the capability to manage and deliver the SQH programme. We will focus particularly on the question of what structures need to be established to ensure that all involved are capable of supporting WBL.

The Scottish Qualification for Headship (SQH)

The SQH project was commissioned to implement a manifesto commitment by the government that 'the strength of a school is critically dependent on the quality of its head. We will establish mandatory qualifications for the post. A headteacher will be appointed only when fully trained to accept responsibility' (Labour Party, 1997). Following consultation, the project was initiated in the autumn of 1997 with a brief to produce a standard for headship in Scottish schools and to design and pilot a qualification based on it. The aim, endorsed by the Minister for Education, was to equip aspiring headteachers to fulfil the key purpose of headship: 'To provide the leadership and management which enables a school to give every pupil high quality education and which promotes the highest possible standards of achievement' (SOEID, 1998a: 3).

The SQH Programme began in 1998 with a pilot developed and managed by the SQH Development Unit funded by the Scottish Office Education and Industry Department (SOEID). In the pilot a small number of participants drawn from six local authorities embarked upon the programme. The following year the programme was launched and half the local authorities in Scotland sponsored participants on the course. After the two-year pilot phase, the management of the SQH programme moved to consortia of universities and local authorities working in partnership. Overall policy-making remained with a national advisory committee chaired by a representative from the Scottish Executive Education Department (SEED), the successor to the SOEID after the establishment of the Scottish Parliament.

The SQH is a two-year development programme for aspiring head-teachers within primary, secondary and special schools leading to both a professional and an academic award: the Post Graduate Diploma in School Leadership and Management (SQH). The programme consists of four units and adopts a mixed mode delivery combining taught elements with WBL, distance learning, peer support and in-school mentoring (see Figure 6.1).

In the consultation document on the SQH programme, *Proposals for Developing a Scottish Qualification for Headship* (SOEID, 1996a), linking individual and organisational development was a clear intention that echoed the concerns of both the government and local authorities who looked for a programme of development that would support school improvement. Critically the type of learning opportunities and assessment tasks included in the programme had to centre on the development and improvement of practice in schools. As a result WBL, in which the candidate would undertake school-based projects that contributed to the school's development, became a focal point of the programme.

In Chapter 5 we proposed that any programme of WBL designed to enhance performance should take into account four essential aspects of learning: reflection on practice, experiential learning, cognitive development and social learning processes. Within the SQH programme, structures were established to facilitate each of these processes:

- *Reflection on practice* Self-evaluation is a process underpinning the programme from the initial self-assessment in Unit 1 to the extended reflective commentaries on the work-based projects in Units 2 and 3.
- *Experiential learning* A substantial proportion of the programme is undertaken in the participant's own school, with the two work-based units being over 60 per cent of the programme.
- *Cognitive development* The participants construct their own learning programme which includes independent study tasks, reading

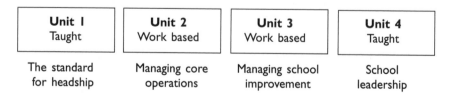

Figure 6.1 Structure of the programme

and other development activities to enhance their knowledge and understanding.

- *Social learning processes* Participants meet regularly with a school-based supporter and, through local authority network meetings with other participants on the programme, discuss their experiences in taking forward the WBL project.

In the next section we will consider how we have addressed each of these aspects in the design of the SQH programme and the implications of this structure for building capability within schools, local authorities and among other providers.

Reflection on practice

Self-evaluation and critical reflection are two key processes in the SQH. When self-evaluation and reflection are used in any programme there is the danger of *reinforcing* poor practice. Therefore, to enable participants to evaluate and review in a balanced and sound manner in order to improve their own performance, two factors are essential. First, there needs be to some type of framework that would delineate and 'measure' aspects of good practice. Secondly, reflection needs to be related to significant experiences and sustained over a lengthy period of time if practitioners are to develop and adapt theories in use (Argyris and Schon, 1974).

For the first of these factors, the Standard for Headship (SHS) is crucial in providing a framework to facilitate reflection on practice. The SHS defines three elements of school leadership and management: professional values, management functions and personal abilities (see Figure 6.2).

A key feature of this construction is the necessary interdependence of the three elements. Reflection against the standard provides the means for participants to explore their professional self, their values and abilities in relation to their performance in carrying out management functions to achieve previously determined outcomes. It is from this interconnectedness of the elements that the SHS derives its power as a tool to support self-evaluation and reflection on practice. The SHS is based upon a general model of practice (Figure 6.3) which could be used to underpin a range of professional standards (Reeves *et al.*, 1998).

Using the SHS as a framework, candidates are asked to address the following questions in their self-evaluation and review:

- Why have you taken a particular course of action? Can you justify your practice?

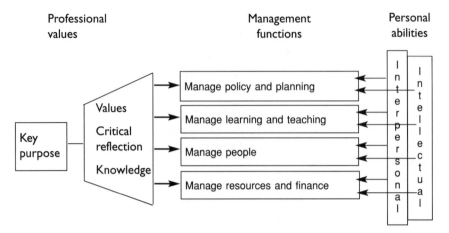

Figure 6.2   The standard for headship
Source: SOEID (1998a: 2)

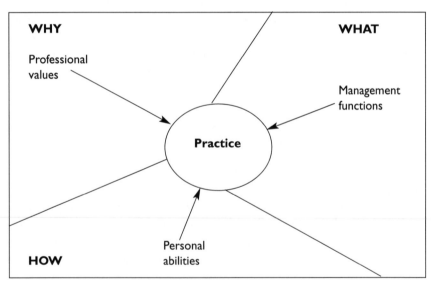

Figure 6.3   Model of professional practice
Source: Reeves *et al.* (1998: 191)

- What functional activities did you use and did they conform with good practice?
- How successfully did you carry out these functions? What has improved as a result?

The second factor, that self-evaluation and reflection are sustained, is ensured by the structure of the SQH programme. Self-evaluation is not simply a one-off preliminary task but is continued through a series of activities over the whole two years. The process begins in Unit 1 with a comprehensive self-assessment using the SHS in which participants evaluate themselves against all three elements of the standard. The outcomes of this exercise are their desired learning outcomes for the next two work-based units.

The process of self-evaluation then continues as participants are required to review their project(s) and to construct, first, a portfolio of evidence that charts the progress and outcomes of the project and, secondly, a commentary that reviews critically the experience of undertaking a programme of WBL and what they have learned as a result.

Experiential learning

For WBL to impact on performance the opportunities for experiential learning must be planned, managed and resourced. Structured opportunities for experimenting with practice in the work situation must be available to the learner. In any WBL programme there are two main tensions: first, between providing an overall structure that has sufficient flexibility to allow participants to work within and contribute positively to the particular context of their school whilst, at the same time, making a worthwhile contribution to their own development. Secondly, the tension between finding ways of structuring learning to ensure the demonstration of competence by learners at a functional level whilst at the same time enabling them to develop their knowledge, understanding and skills.

Alternative ways of organising WBL have been developed to try to resolve these tensions. One way is to break down relevant areas of activity into small items of behaviour. The critical factor here is to identify likely opportunities for the participant to exhibit each of the specific behaviours. However, this atomistic approach, with aspects of practice described as small discrete items, is liable to obscure any sense of how these specific behaviours can link together to achieve an outcome or that action is based on a wider set of intentions and purposes other than merely demonstrating behaviours defined by the standard.

The second way of organising WBL is to develop a more holistic approach to the development of practice, which is the strategy adopted in the SQH. Participants in the SQH programme are not simply practising isolated skills (for instance, chairing a meeting). Instead, participants must take forward a substantial development project in the school that is clearly based on a set of educationally justifiable intentions and that is conducted over an extended period of time. Rather than seeking opportunities to practise discrete skills, the process of taking forward a substantial development provides the means for developing skills, knowledge and understanding in a more connected way. This holistic approach still needs some means of ensuring coherence and structure that, in the SQH programme, is provided by the SHS which is used as both a planning and an evaluation tool. The structure of the SHS has proved to be useful way of breaking learning down into manageable units while at the same time maintaining overall coherence.

In the SHS the management functions cover the four key functions of managing teaching and learning, people, policy and planning, resources and finance. In Unit 2 participants have to undertake a whole-school management project that enables them to cover the key functions of managing teaching, learning and people, while the project in Unit 3 covers the key functions of managing policy and planning, and resources and finance. Each management function is broken down into core activities and then into tasks. The core activities are used as the basis for the planning and evaluation of the school-based project (see Figure 6.4).

The intention of any project is not simply to achieve an end product (for example, produce a policy document), but to engage the candidate in the processes of management. The use of the core activities to plan, develop and review learning means the management processes are fully taken into consideration alongside the achievement and demonstration of the specified outcomes (see Table 6.1).

Approaching WBL in this way places substantial responsibility on the participant to 'make things work', to be flexible, to work with others, to deal with difficulties in order to find solutions and to achieve the planned outcomes. Equally, appropriate opportunities for the learner to develop and practise new skills must be available. Involvement in a WBL programme needs to be regarded as a legitimate part of provision for staff development within the school that contributes to its improvement agenda. For this reason it is important there is a strong link between the learning opportunities provided for the learner and organisational needs. Participants must be able to work within and contribute to the ongoing school improvement agenda using their projects to take forward specific development priorities. In the case of the SQH, since the candidates are aspirant head-teachers, they must be involved in leading and managing substantial

Key functions

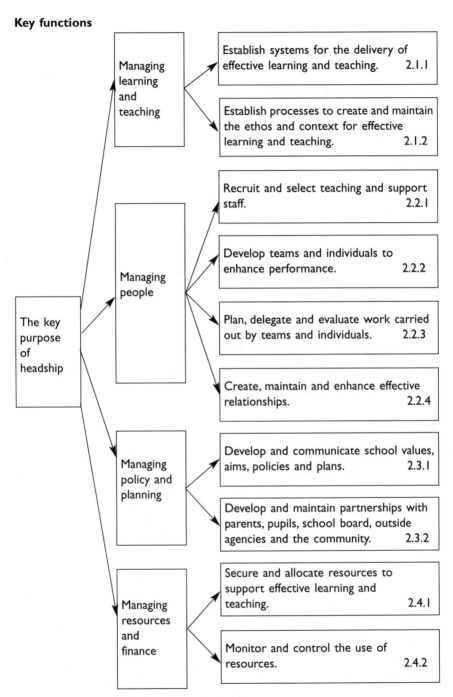

Figure 6.4   Key functions and core activities
Source: SOEID (1998a: 6)

Table 6.1 Planning a project

Unit 2: Review and development of health education programme	
Task	Core activity
Discussion with HT and SMT	2.2.3/2.2.4
Establishment and leadership of primary/secondary working group	2.2.3/2.2.4
Discussion with co-ordinators for health education, pastoral care and PSE programmes	2.1.1/2.2.3
Review of current provision for health education in science and PSE programmes	2.1.1
Feedback to staff and identification of targets	2.2.3/2.2.4
Planning, implementation and evaluation of staff development programme: school-based and local authority programmes	2.2.2
Creation of planning format for differentiated programmes of study for health education	2.1.1
Development of assessment tasks for each stage	2.1.1
Implementation and monitoring of pupil learning	2.1.1
Planning, implementation and evaluation of Be Safe School initiative	2.1.2/2.2.2
Evaluation of project	2.2.3/2.2.4

projects that have a whole-school (rather than a departmental) focus.

It might be argued that linking organisational and personal development in this way is restrictive and unduly limits learners' choices, preventing any lateral thinking and flair on their part. Ideally, perhaps, learners should have an open choice and be allowed to play to their strengths. But this viewpoint is misguided, first, because participants must always work within the context of a specific school at a particular moment in its history and share responsibility with the rest of the staff for the outcomes of the school's work and, secondly, if they are working to a standard they have to meet the full range of outcomes it specifies.

Undoubtedly, there is a tension between the needs and aspirations of the individual learner and the collective needs of the organisation that raises ethical questions relating to the purpose and ownership of the project that need to be considered by both the participant and those managing the programme. If participants are to contribute to their schools' development, working collaboratively must be a central focus but, for this collaboration to be possible, there must be:

- negotiation between the head, the learner and the staff group;
- agreed outcomes for the project;
- resourcing of the project, including staff time;
- opportunities for delegation giving staff responsibilities in relation to the project; and
- other staff actively participating in the project.

Thus the provision of experiential learning within the school requires, first, a particular set of attitudes towards staff development where the mutual dependence of staff and school development is recognised and valued and, secondly, investment to support a positive outcome for the participant and the school.

There is the practical question about how many staff undertaking substantial WBL programmes any one school can sustain. More contentiously there is the question of the well-being of the individual learner. On the SQH, leading and managing a substantial whole-school project is a very public affair. In settings where there is resistance to collaborative working this can expose participants to huge pressures and possibly failure. The nature of the context in which a participant works is a vital consideration where the school is used as the site for learning.

Differences between schools

The issue of context raises practical concerns as well as ethical considerations. Schools differ in their size, geographical location and cultural climate and so participants will be working in contexts that vary dramatically. These differences pose a range of questions about the provision of opportunities for experiential learning as well as equality of opportunity for learners. For instance, on the SQH programme a group of candidates can include a deputy head in a large primary in the suburbs, an assistant head in an inner-city comprehensive, a class teacher in a two-teacher school in a rural area or a co-ordinator of a special education unit. Within such a mixed group the opportunities to engage in whole-school management activities will vary enormously.

Differences in ideologies may also have a significant impact upon the opportunities to engage in the range of management functions. There is an obvious contrast between the traditional subject specialism orientation of the secondary school and the ideology of child-centred approaches in the primary sector. Another lies between mainstream schools and special schools or units where the strength of care and welfare is important. It might be argued that, as all schools increasingly conform to prescribed standards and performance measures, there will be less diversity. However, currently schools remain significantly different in their capacity to provide the necessary opportunities that participants need while, at the same time, addressing the school's development needs.

In the key function of managing teaching and learning there are significant sectoral differences. The subject specialisms and departmental structures that have traditionally existed in secondary schools have meant that issues related to teaching and learning and the curriculum have been dealt with historically at departmental level. One of the points of debate that has been raised about the SQH programme is: what does managing teaching and learning mean in a secondary school at senior-management level?

Within the primary sector a different tradition has existed where many headteachers have regarded themselves as the 'lead teacher', often relying quite heavily on demonstrations of their teaching skill, working very closely with children alongside teachers, introducing curriculum change by being the main developer of curricular programmes. For many participants from the primary sector dealing with an increasing array of strategic tasks in policy and development planning and financial management has not fitted easily with this tradition. Even in larger primary settings, management may still be on a fairly informal level, with the emphasis on activities such as collaborative teaching or day-to-day discussions. The evidence-based approach in the SQH programme contrasts with this practice in placing a greater emphasis on establishing baselines, success criteria, gathering evidence and evaluating outcomes that can cause problems in the schools of some participants.

Development is also handled differently across the sectors. An example of the contrast between primary and secondary is exemplified by characteristic approaches to managing a change project found by Reeves (1999) in her study of change leadership. Sector differences in how change is taken forward are evident particularly in relation to delegation, which was found to be a real issue in primaries. In the primary sector change is often championed and led directly by the headteacher. In the secondary sector, on the other hand, the headteacher generally shares responsibility within a senior management team whose members often have to engage in lobbying and building of agreement among the departments in order to seek consonance between departmental and whole-school policy, and delegate responsibilities across different levels in the school.

The school's external environment is equally important in taking a work-based project forward. Again in the SQH programme we have found differences in terms of context and opportunities posed by the urban/suburban/rural location of the school that will shape learning opportunities for participants. If we take one area of management we can illustrate some of the ways in which location can shape practice. Partnerships with parents and the wider community are now key areas of activity within schools in Scotland identified in the set of performance indicators used in the inspection of schools (SOEID, 1996b) that demand the attention of school managers and leaders. However, how that is operationalised may be very different in different geographical locations. In rural schools – both primary and secondary –long-established communities may demand a different level of interaction and accountability than is evident in other schools. Partnership in an urban environment such as an inner-city area may contrast dramatically and again demand different strategies to engage parents in their children's education. Size and location may also limit the choices within the curriculum. It is therefore vital that participants work within the mission and aims of their particular school and contribute to the school's efforts to achieve these aims.

Achieving legitimacy for the WBL within a specific context

This degree of diversity has highlighted the importance of particularity in planning work-based interventions. The starting point needs to be the school's mission and aims. Participants must be able to justify their projects in terms of underpinning purposes and a clear relationship to enabling their schools to be better able to achieve their mission and aims. Learners need to start by analysing the particular context in which they work and seeking appropriate sets of action to bring about improvement on the basis of their analysis. Participants need to consider how they will go about the work-based project in the context in which they work. They need to consider their strategies for implementation in the light of:

- the size and organisation of the school; and
- the sector and geographical location.

Equally important is the development history of the school:

- What have been the recent developments that have or have not been successful in the school?
- What are the current initiatives?
- What in the culture of the school supports improvement, particularly the school's overall approach to the management of change?

What we have found in the SQH programme is that it is important not to consider the context as a limiting factor preventing a learner from experiencing areas of professional practice but, rather, to ensure that due account is taken of the genuine circumstances in which the learner works. What participants are asked to achieve is a whole-school project, and 'whole schoolness' varies according to context as do the expected outcomes of any particular project (see Table 6.2).

Cognitive development

In the SQH programme participants are required to develop with as much clarity as possible a plan for what they were going 'to do' in school. The majority of projects on the pilot were commendably planned in a great deal of detail, breaking each area into very small items. However, these first efforts were very much action plans: participants identified tasks, steps, success criteria, resources, time line. This approach emphasised task completion and gave little space to ideas about learning and development. Indeed, these initial plans reflected a constant concern about WBL that it tends to be inward

Table 6:2   Achieving a whole-school focus

Participant	Focus	Whole schoolness
AHT, primary early years remit	Introducing early numeracy	Development of an action plan to develop a whole-school policy on mathematics
AHT, secondary liaison remit	Primary/secondary curriculum liaison	Consultation on liaison across the curriculum
AHT, co-ordinator, special needs unit	Literacy programme for pupils with language and communication disorders	Integration of approaches in the whole-school literacy policy and programme

looking and parochial and the importance of ideas from outside the organisation tends to be ignored, often being dismissed as simply 'theoretical' with little relevance to practice.

This divide between practice and wider ideas was evident in the rationales produced by the majority of candidates on the pilot for their work-based projects. There was relatively little engagement with educational purposes or principles of management and leadership. Instead there was a tendency to justify the specific project largely in terms of operationalising local authority and national priorities rather than on the basis of purposes and principles relevant to the education of pupils in the particular school. It seemed as if purposes and principles were associated with the taught components and reading was regarded as an activity to be undertaken solely for the completion of the written assignment. This location of theory and educational values within the taught elements limited the potential of experiential learning, not only because there was a rather superficial engagement with values and purposes but also the potential of reading to open up alternatives for action through access to new ideas and sources of information was lost.

In order to create an awareness of the importance of ideas, this traditional dichotomy between theory and practice and the privileging of one or the other needs to be challenged. MacIntyre (1997), when addressing the perennial tension in the development of student teachers between academic learning and practice in schools, challenges the place given to theoretical learning. He argues that in initial teacher education theoretical learning has been traditionally privileged and the power of the experiences and ideas of students was ignored. He proposed a model of student learning in which the learner is able to draw from a range of sources to seek solutions to problems they find in their practice and to use this range of sources to interrogate ideas and their own practice. A similar model is followed in the SQH programme. Although the emphasis in WBL is placed on 'process knowledge' (Eraut, 1994) – that is, the knowledge the learners derive from reflecting upon their practice – access to other sources, particularly theoretical bodies of knowledge, is equally important if that process knowledge is to be developed and elaborated.

Clear links between experience and cognitive development are needed. In shaping WBL it is important to create opportunities to enable the learners to consider not just alternative ways of carrying out a task but to make connections between purposes and values, strategies adopted and theoretical principles in order that they can work effectively in different contexts. We drew from previous work on WBL agreements (Thompson *et al.*, 1996). From an initial idea about requiring participants to draw up a study calendar, we developed a 'learning plan' that encompassed a wide view of learning and a variety of experiences and activities within which the practical project was one element. In the learning plan participants consider what opportunities, tasks, experiences, and sources of ideas they would want to access in order to ensure coverage of the relevant sections of the three elements of the SHS: professional values (which included values, knowledge and understanding), management functions and personal abilities.

Developing the learning plan helped us develop a more holistic view of learning and it strengthens the link between the taught and the experiential elements whilst providing a structure to enable learners not just to link theory to practice but also to theorise about practice. Planning learning opportunities in this way is also a means of overcoming the limitations of specific contexts. Learners may not be able to access readily areas of practice, such as recruitment and selection or the management of the whole-school budget in their own establishment. As part of the learning plan, opportunities outside the participant's own school (such as training, simulation or shadowing) can be identified and planned. Personal skills training areas need to be addressed, such as:

- assertiveness;
- communication skills;
- interviewing techniques;
- conflict resolution;
- problem-solving skills; and
- teamwork strategies.

To maximise the potential of the learning plan, access to resources is a vital consideration, particularly when participants may work at some distance from facilities such as university libraries. On the SQH programme a range of strategies have been developed to support participants such as open-learning units, including study tasks, reading guides and access to key texts through local authority or school-based resource centres. Increasingly those managing and providing WBL will be able to use net-based solutions to providing access to these types of resources.

Social processes: support systems

Joyce and Showers (1988) point to the importance of opportunities for learners to practise and receive feedback about their performance. Reflective practice cannot be a solitary experience; opportunities to explore, analyse and discuss experience and insights are vital.

The question of support for WBL was critical in the design of the SQH. On a practical level there is the question of sustaining participants when they are remote from other participants and from the support of tutors. On a more fundamental level there is the question of how to provide genuine opportunities for the learner to reflect critically upon practice in ways that enable him or her to theorise. This issue of isolation is particularly pertinent for aspiring headteachers where there is usually only one, or at most two, participants in any school. For other groups of staff in the school there is a greater possibility of building in collegial approaches of support for WBL. In designing the SQH, however, we were conscious of the position of individual candidates so we had to consider the development of a network of support. This network of support included school support and wider support structures delivered by the employer and the provider. Let us examine each of these in turn.

In-school support

In-school mentoring was seen as the most useful approach as it would provide opportunities for the learner to work with a more experienced manager and also provide instant access. In a work-based programme that predates the SQH, the Management Competences Scheme, Reeves and Forde (1994) found that, particularly in primary schools, the mentoring process helped to develop a team approach within the senior management team. Forde (1998: 15), in her evaluation of a similar scheme where all mentors were headteachers, found this group saw mentoring as 'a vehicle to work together on a professional relationship – a working relationship with a clear focus on what to do'. Drawing from these previous evaluations, headteachers were identified as the most likely supporters for SQH candidates. In a sense this emphasised and extended a role headteachers would normally be expected to undertake in relation to their senior staff.

The discussions with the supporter provide important opportunities for participants not just to plan and reflect upon specific strategies and explore what makes effective practice, but also to express concerns and feelings about their role as a senior manager, as an aspiring headteacher – in some ways to 'think themselves into headship'. The findings of an evaluation study of the role of the supporter in the SQH by Simpson *et al.*, (2000) illustrate that the majority of learners and supporters viewed supporters as a vital part of the programme. The supporters characterised their role as having:

- motivated learners
- listened to problems
- acted as a critical friend
- made it possible for learners to carry out the project
- provided invaluable on-hand help and advice
- provided insight into context
- been a sounding board
- helped to identify practical projects for the SQH from the SDP [school development plan] (*ibid.*: 14).

Most of the items listed above suggest a notion of mentoring as 'critical friendship'. However the last item ('helped to identify practical projects for the SQH from the SDP') points to the importance of the power and influence of the in-school supporter in facilitating WBL opportunities. From the experiences of participants having difficulty in taking forward work-based projects, the role of mentor as sponsor is equally as important as that of critical friend. At the outset, sponsorship for entry to the programme is necessary and thereafter access to resources, time, areas of responsibility and activities has to be facilitated. Lack of sponsorship has been a significant block on the quality of opportunities for experiential learning available for some candidates on the SQH. This experience suggests that the mentor needs to be someone who is willing to support the participant and who has sufficient status and power to make the provision of learning opportunities possible.

Though mentoring is a demanding role there were likely to be benefits to the supporter as well as the learner. Forde (1998) found that some mentors commented that their work in mentoring had helped them become more structured in planning and carrying out management tasks and to become more self-critical. A similar outcome has been found in the SQH. In the evaluation conducted by Simpson *et al.*, (2000) into the role of the supporter in the SQH, over 67 per cent of supporters reported the benefits of acting as a supporter outweighed the difficulties they encountered. The types of benefits being noted by Simpson *et al.*, (*ibid.*: 24) echo the findings of the previous evaluations and include:

- made me reflect on my own practice;
- forces me to think and focus more on the task in hand;
- allowed me to step back and look at planning from a different angle;
- offered challenges and alternatives to current practice;
- its updated me on current trends and research;

- increased my motivation to revisit the bones of our remit;
- having to take a more objective stance on school issues;
- being a supporter has helped me to analyse a great deal of what I do professionally; and
- refreshing my mind on certain issues.

There are difficulties in conflating the role of headteacher and supporter automatically. Mentoring, in some extreme cases, can become a narrow view of role modelling where the learner feels under pressure to copy the style and behaviour of the supporter (McMahon, 1996). There are also other difficulties, such as increased dependency or reinforcement of poor or outdated modes of practice, clashes of personality, difficulties in the professional relationship between head and learner (for example, significant differences in style and values), which will militate against the effectiveness of this role.

The role of supporter/mentor does demand an open-ended approach in which the focus is on the learner's needs and on creating opportunities for learners to review practice. There needs to be a clear understanding by the supporter of the programme in relation to both the impact of the project on the school and the needs of the individual participant. Within the SQH training of the supporter is an important element providing guidance about developing open-ended approaches to mentoring, including the range of interpersonal skills, such as focusing, active listening and problem-solving techniques. A framework for support is mapped out to match the development of the WBL project in school with formal meetings set at various stages of the project, such as planning, ongoing review and evaluation (Figure 6.5).

Wider support structures

Within the SQH programme the role of the in-school supporter is complemented by others. The two who are most involved are a university tutor who delivers the taught elements and provides academic support through tutorials and seminars and a local authority co-ordinator who manages the recruitment and selection process, the training of supporters and arranges for network meetings of learners where they explore common issues arising from their experiences in taking forward the work-based projects. There is also a field assessor who shares the assessment role with the tutor. The different relationships are mapped out in Figure 6.6.

An underpinning principle in the arrangements for support in the SQH programme is to recognise and support the learner's access to

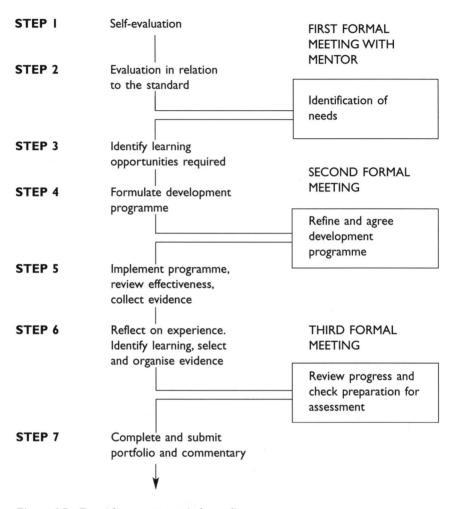

Figure 6.5 Providing support (adapted)
Source: Reeves *et al.* (1998: 188)

a range of perspectives by securing opportunities for cognitive development and social learning. The relationship between the different types of knowledge (what is traditionally viewed as the theory/practice divide) is also reflected in the structural arrangements and provision:

- *Taught elements* A university tutor will work with an associate tutor (who is either a headteacher or a local authority adviser) to deliver the course.
- *Work-based element* Supported by an open-learning programme

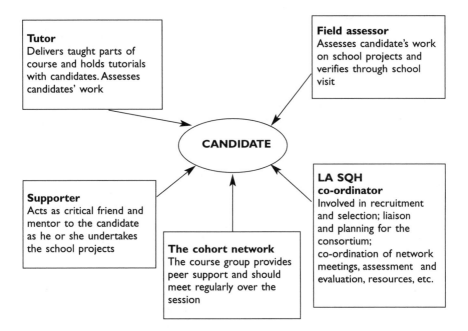

Figure 6.6   The SQH programme: roles and responsiblities

and guided reading of academic material.
- *The assessment process*   The university tutor and a field assessor (a headteacher or local authority adviser) work collaboratively to produce a summative assessment for the work-based elements.
- *Local authority co-ordinator and university tutor*   Collaborate to manage a WBL programme that ensures access to a suitable work environment as well as arrange and structure a range of other learning opportunities.

The close involvement of the local authority in providing support goes back to the purposes of the programme in linking personal professional development to school improvement. The close association of the local authority in supporting the programme helps ensure the needs of the employers are also served.

If the intention of improving practice for the benefit of the school and its pupils is to be served, all partners need to be able to deliver effectively the elements they are responsible for. However, this is an area often overlooked at the outset. Within the pilot project the importance of building capacity in the educational system to sustain the programme emerged as a central concern. The training of all involved in the programme was one strategy – with courses for co-ordinators, tutors, assessors and supporters in addition to their active involvement in the trialling, development and management of the programme through various working groups and forums.

Building this capability has been vital for the SQH programme but we are only now beginning to consider the impact of this development on those involved in schools, in the local authorities and in the universities. The close linking of local authorities and universities through consortia is one instance and it will be worth considering over time the impact of these structures on both groups. For the local authorities there are many issues that will need to be explored. What does it mean for a local authority to gather a cohort of potential heads and work with them over a sustained period? What is the impact of having heads and others in the authority acting as supporters or as trained field assessors and working with the next group of heads within an authority?

The SQH programme has also shaped relationships between local authorities and the providers, in this instance the universities. Funding for the programme has gone to the local authorities, so the universities have entered into partnerships with local authorities to deliver and manage the programme. For the universities increasing their capability of working with students at a distance from the university has been significant. The universities have had to establish infrastructures to work with the local authorities to provide access to resources, support in-school development and access to opportunities for development outside the school. Increasingly there is the development of net-based support, particularly email. More fundamentally a significant national programme such as the SQH has helped to increase the legitimacy of the site of the school as a context for learning and WBL as a method of professional development worthy of academic recognition.

Resource implications

On the face of it, it might seem that WBL is a less costly option with the candidate remaining in school undertaking a substantial development project that will contribute to the school's improvement agenda. Given our previous discussion about the improvement of practice through structured opportunities for development, WBL has been regarded as the most effective approach in the SQH. However, it needs to be emphasised this approach has significant resource implications.

Throughout this chapter we have emphasised the importance of WBL being structured and managed. Equally important is the provision of resources. Resourcing is a vital part of the development of strategy in relation to the introduction of WBL at school, local authority and nationally at governmental level because there are significant costs involved in building the capability of the various partners. Developing the infrastructures for managing and delivering the programme and the specific training for each of the roles within the programme (in the case of the SQH, for the co-ordinators, university tutors, associate tutors, supporters and field assessors) have required a significant commitment on the part of all those involved.

To maintain the programme at school level the planning of the development project that is the basis for the WBL programme needs to include resources for the participant to be able to conduct the project successfully, including engaging in development activities, any materials or support, such as administrative assistance. For a number of participants with class commitments particularly in the primary sector, limitations on the amount of time being available to take the project forward has been a critical issue. Time also has to be made available for the involvement of other staff in the development activities, such as membership of working groups, participation in in-service activities, contributing to consultation tasks and evaluations. Time for both the candidate and other staff often has to be facilitated through the provision of cover.

Resourcing at both school and local authority level needs to include a range of areas if the programme is to have the desired effect of enhancing practice. These are detailed in the Table 6.3.

The local authority has a significant role to play in programmes like the SQH. Activities such as briefing potential candidates, recruitment and selection, the organisation of local network meetings for learners, co-ordination of local authority personnel acting as supporters, field assessors and associate tutors are undertaken and managed by an SQH co-ordinator within the local authority. This role has significant cost implications, as do the other activities the local authorities undertake in managing the programme as members of joint management groups in partnership with the providers (see Table 6.4).

Conclusions

In this chapter we have mapped out quite an elaborate system that has been created to support a particular programme, but this has

Table 6.3 Supporting a participant: resourcing implications

Area	Resources
Course fees	Fees per candidate to the provider
Cover costs	Time during the school day for candidates to take forward project, particularly if have class commitments
Staff time	Cover costs to enable other staff to be involved in the development project during the school day; time supporter/learner meetings
Travel	Costs for travel to attend taught elements and events such as local network meetings with other learners
Books and other materials	Access to set tests and other materials related to the programme
ICT	Use of ICT for support and delivery – access to ICT resources with sufficient capability

Table 6.4 Resource implications for local authorities

Area	Resources
Co-ordination	Staff costs to cover range of activities within the local authority
Assessment	Staff and cover costs for field assessors
Training	Costs of training for all school and LEA staff involved: supporters, field assessors, associate tutors and co-ordinators
Access to resources	Books and other materials available centrally; development of net-based support

served to illustrate some of the structural implications of adopting WBL as a basis for improving performance at a variety of levels.

For schools:

• Linking of individual needs with organisational needs using standards to provide a bridge to enable this link to work.

- Adopting a new mindset in relation to CPD and looking carefully at the learning opportunities available in the workplace.
- Linking internal opportunities with external opportunities and support to promote the development of competence.
- Developing the capacity for coaching and mentoring within a school.

For local authorities

- Changing role from that of provider of staff development to that of facilitator of WBL and access to learning support for school-based staff.
- Enhancing their role as developers of learning capability within the schools and the authority.
- Helping school staff to gain access to new ideas and to social learning processes through opportunities to interact with a range of people: other learners, other schools and organisations. Access to information.

For providers

- Creating new ways of working together with local authorities and schools.
- Developing effective support for WBL.
- Flexing delivery systems, assessment processes and accreditation to meet the needs of schools and employers.

7

Improving performance: the learners' view

Introduction

Having looked at some of the structural implications of work-based learning (WBL), we now want to explore the experience of those who are involved in a work-based approach to developing practice. In part this is to serve as an exploration of some of the theoretical ideas outlined in Chapter 4 as well to provide some feedback on the operation of the various elements of WBL from experienced teachers.

We are again focusing on the Scottish Qualification for Headship (SQH) and our justification for doing so is the evidence the course is having an effect on practice in schools (Reeves *et al.*, forthcoming). In response to a survey by external evaluators, candidates described changes in the following areas of their work (Simpson *et al.*, 2000):

- a sharper focus on outcomes;
- more thorough planning; and
- improved monitoring and evaluation.

Their headteachers also identified positive effects for:

- the candidates' practice;
- the senior management team in the school; and
- the whole school, including the staff, the parents, the pupils and the wider community.

The bulk of the evidence is taken from the first cohort of 164 candidates on the SQH. Although this group has not yet completed the course, the consistency of the themes emerging from their evidence and the evaluations of the pilot make the initial results of our investigations into their experience worth reporting as they throw an interesting light on the issues of WBL and performance.

The material is organised into two main sections. The first of these explores candidates' views of what has contributed to their learning in terms of various structures that were put in place to support their development:

- taking action;
- using the standard for headship;
- the place of reading;
- the role of self-evaluation; and
- support in the workplace.

The second section concentrates on the nature of the learning that has taken place that shows how matters of performance are closely embedded in the particular context in which the learner works. The areas covered in this section are:

- developing knowledge;
- identity and power; and
- accounting for change.

Finally we will summarise what the evidence seems to suggest about the four major elements of WBL we identified in Chapter 5 and about the model for improving practice we proposed in Chapter 4.

Background

The data for this chapter are drawn from a variety of sources. Most of it has been generated as the result of a research project to investigate the learning of candidates and the impact of their participation in the SQH programme on the schools where they work (Reeves *et al.*, forthcoming). This has involved analysing the Unit 2 commentaries from a representative sample of 40 candidates, submitted in the summer of 2000. Twenty of these candidates have also been interviewed about their experience of the course, the outcomes of their project work in school and their perceptions of their own learning.

In addition we have drawn on three independent studies of the programme:

- An initial evaluation of the pilot in 1999, which concentrated on the learning and experiences of 54 candidates on both the accelerated route (where candidates claimed for prior experiential learning) and the standard route (where they were actively engaged in structured WBL) (Morris, 1999).
- Two further small-scale evaluations in 2000 looking at the effects of having a candidate in school, the role of the supporter (Simpson

et al., 2000) and the costs (Malcolm and Wilson, 2000). These two evaluations concentrated on the experiences of the 164 candidates enrolled on the standard route in 1999.

We are also using candidates' comments in response to an evaluation of Unit 2 conducted in late summer 2000. Candidates were surveyed using four open-ended questions about the benefits and drawbacks of undertaking the course.

In looking at participants' responses to the programme it is probably worth reminding ourselves of those features of the SQH that have a particular bearing on learning. First, there is the model of practice in the Standard for Headship (SHS) with its three interconnecting –elements:

1) Professional values.
2) Management functions.
3) Professional abilities.

The purpose of this design is to foster self-evaluation and critical reflection since it entails that competence is tested by asking the following questions:

- Did the action undertaken by the practitioner embody good practice (as defined by the standard)?
- Can the practitioner justify his or her action on the basis of professionally defensible values and in terms of purpose?
- Did the practitioner have the professional abilities necessary to achieve a demonstrable improvement in targeted outcomes?

These questions open up the issue of competence to professional judgement because intentions and contextual bases for decision-making become a crucial part of assessment. The framework for assessment for the programme therefore requires candidates to offer 'critical self-assessment' and 'Critical commentary on practical project/s and reflection on learning and personal development' (SOEID, 1998c: 9), in addition to presenting a portfolio of evidence illustrating the successful completion of whole-school management tasks in school.

Secondly, the SQH offers candidates a variety of opportunities to learn through the following:

1) Evaluating themselves against the SHS.
2) Accessing a body of knowledge about school leadership and management through reading, oral input from speakers, tutorials.
3) Undertaking leadership and management projects in school designed to allow them to develop and demonstrate practical competence.

4) Discussing their practice with their mentors, peers and tutors.
5) Preparing portfolios of evidence and commentaries on their work that meet the terms for competence as defined in the SHS.

Using this mixed approach to professional development we hoped to avoid promoting a mechanistic form of competence. In this sense the SQH programme might be said to focus on 'expertise' as opposed to 'competence' in that it addresses the 'softer skills' (for example vision, interpersonal skills, analytical skills) encompassing both specific abilities and ways of organising knowledge (Konrad, 1998).

The SQH seeks to enable candidates to explore personal, technical, contextual and theoretical understandings of school leadership and management. Crucially, it encourages and supports candidates in making sense of these in an interconnected and holistic way in the hope this will enable them to operate in a context that will require they:

- cope with high levels of uncertainty
- explore the future
- anticipate and manage change
- operate effectively in a political context
- take responsibility for managing one's own development (Freedman, 1998: 2).

The experience of learning

Taking action

The evaluation returns on Unit 2 (the first of the work-based stages in the SQH programme) showed an overwhelmingly positive response to WBL with over 85 per cent of the primary sector sample identifying this as the most positive aspect of the course. Enthusiasm in the secondary sector was more muted with only 50 per cent identifying WBL as the main benefit. The following sample of comments indicates the advantages identified by those who endorsed the approach:

> Tests whether you can get round, through difficulties. Putting values, thoughts, strategies into action. Work based tasks do make the learning easier. The learning has a direct impact on practice which straight theoretical can't. I liked the combination of the practical management experience combined with the research required to be reflective. I enjoyed the independence to study and feel that it led to an immediate

improvement in my professional skills and knowledge. Whole staff were easily involved and were more supportive because they had been involved in consultation. Developing the knowledge and skills of others (Unit 2 evaluations).

What was also interesting in these returns was that the theme of working with others came through so strongly as both a source of satisfaction and as a novel experience. One of the common early criticisms of the SHS was that it did not place enough emphasis on teamwork and participation. Having analysed the commentaries and the interview transcripts it seems that real engagement in decision-making on the part of staff in schools is less common than we would have predicted. Maybe this reflects that experience and understanding of group processes amongst school managers remains quite weak in a significant number of schools, despite all the pressure of recent changes.

The returns showed that 39 per cent of the primary respondents identified the opportunity to lead and manage school projects as a benefit of the course, whereas secondary candidates (60 per cent) were more likely to point to the benefits of reading, coursework and discussion.

This may well reflect the rather different levels of opportunities for gaining management experience that prevail between the two sectors. In the secondary schools, people generally serve quite lengthy apprenticeships in a number of promoted posts whereas, in primary, there are fewer rungs on the ladder and the dominant role of headteachers may mean that even deputy heads have little direct experience of whole-school management (Southworth, 1995):

> The one aspect that I have got most out of was the fact that I had to take on sole responsibility for the development of one aspect of the school's development plan over the session. I would have been heavily involved in that as a matter of course but the fact that I was in 'full charge' gave me a lot of opportunities that maybe I would not have had otherwise to develop myself and my own beliefs and views further (Unit 2 commentary).

This also applied in some secondary schools, particularly in relation to certain aspects of management relevant to Unit 3 where there was also a stronger emphasis on adopting a strategic approach to development:

> I wasn't involved with previously, had no experience of finance and I have managed to get myself sucked into that through this project. That might not have happened without SQH and it was a major gap in my

portfolio – the HT is much keener for me to work closely with him on school budgeting now (interview).

The vividness of the experience of WBL is apparent in the interviews carried out to investigate candidates' experience of the course. It was clear many candidates felt challenged by undertaking their projects and that it was very important to them they were seen as doing something of benefit to the school: 'It definitely did [have an outcome] – the maths results went up. They [the children] felt much more confident too because they were doing bigger things mentally and they were more confident in written work. It raised their confidence and that raised their ability' (interview).

Benefit to the school is also a key feature of the written feedback from the evaluation of Unit 2, as can be seen from this collection of comments:

> Witnessing improvement in attainment. Working closely with some staff and seeing the development of writing and the success of it [the project]. Improvement in the school's approach to learning and teaching. It has given the SMT a clearer sense of direction. Meaningful exercise which has benefited not only the department but the whole school. Developing confidence of staff (Unit 2 evaluations).

This theme of achievement and gaining greater control over the quality of one's work is important. In a sense the SQH provides many participants with powerful and detailed feedback on their performance both through the conduct of the school-based projects and through the formal assessment procedures. Given the relatively low level of implementation of personal review processes in Scottish schools this could explain why this has been a vivid experience for a number of candidates.

There is also the broader issue of efficacy. It is obviously essential, if the qualification is to have any currency, that candidates and their colleagues regard the SHS as a valid standard. Its credibility depends on its use being seen to result in worthwhile outcomes.

The key features of using experiential project work as a vehicle for learning emerging from this feedback seem to be as follows:

- WBL offered learners the chance to achieve, and be seen to achieve, positive outcomes for the school.
- Many participants enjoyed taking on the challenge and responsibility of the tasks.
- Learners found the realism and practicality of this way of learning made it more meaningful to them.

- The majority remarked that working closely with their colleagues had been both rewarding and productive.

Working with the standard

The favourable responses to WBL and assertions of the efficacy of the standard sit alongside what seems, on the face of it, a puzzling observation on the part of a significant number of the interviewees. The experience of 'doing' the course is described in almost coercive terms. This impression comes from the interviews where expressions such as 'it forces you', 'it makes you' or 'the SQH pushes you' are used in discussing the effects of the course. What candidates seem to be identifying is that working towards the standard constrains them to act in certain ways: 'I really think when doing the project I would not have been able to resist the temptation to cut corners if I had not been doing the SQH' (interview).

So what is it that leads people to make these kinds of assertions? There is not an entirely clear answer as yet but there are clues pointing to two mechanisms embedded in the assessment process. The requirements to:

1) have evidence the project brought about improvement and was carried out in accordance with the SHS.
2) justify actions.

There are three occasions in the WBL process where, if candidates are to prepare successfully for assessment, they need to engage with the standard and make sense of it. These are outlined in Figure 7.1 (U1–U3):

1) Matching the tasks they are going to undertake in school to the standard.
2) Identifying the evidence that will demonstrate they have successfully carried out the activities specified in the standard.
3) Selecting and organising their evidence to demonstrate their competence.

The diagram necessarily simplifies the process in a way that obscures the dynamic interaction between the cognitive operations involved in completing each of these stages and action in the school. Our evidence suggests it is impossible to untangle whether behaviour leads to an understanding of the standard or whether understanding the standard leads to behaviour. Sense-making seems to be very much a cyclical and iterative process: in carrying out each stage of the project there

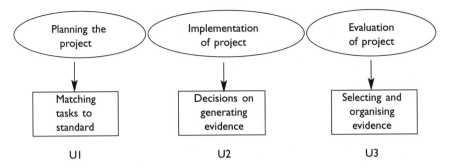

Figure 7.1 Preparing for the portfolio

is a need for candidates to reconstruct their experience in a specific form for an external audience so action and understanding constantly sit side by side.

The effects of these processes are strongly evidenced in the interview data, with more than 75 per cent of the participants claiming that being on the SQH has changed the way they think about school leadership, often along the lines indicated by the following respondent in the first evaluation: 'Up till now it was just something I did, I didn't really think about it as managing, I just did it and then I went on and did the next thing' (Morris and Reeves, 2000: 528).

For those who have already had a more formal introduction to management the main claim for changing their practice is that they have moved away from a very task-focused approach to one where there is a greater commitment to working with and through people and on underlying purposes. Again, this echoes the suspicion hinted at in the first section of this discussion that there is still a great deal of administration going on in schools. This is possibly underlined by the emphasis candidates place on teamworking and delegation as areas where their practice and assumptions have changed.

The phrases most frequently used to describe the experience of using the standard are as follows:

> It has given me a structure/a framework for analysing/checking out what I want to do. I used to be instinctive now I stop before I make decisions/I choose from options. I look at management in a different way. It has helped me firm up my ideas, make my philosophy clearer (interviews).

For these candidates it seems that the combination of project management and the need to meet the SHS is a powerful, though not necessarily comfortable, experience:

The SQH has made me reflect on my behaviour, my management style and maybe I have modified things I do as a result. You are evaluating, you are thinking more about what you're doing and why you're doing it. You think more about your approach and your values in doing it (interviews).

Why might the SHS have this power? The following quotation gives several possible hints:

I have found the information in 'The Standard for Headship in Scotland' text to be of great help. It has helped focus my thoughts on the work I was doing and has helped to justify to myself that it was right to do some of the things in a particular way. I think it would be fair to say that a lot of information in the booklet reflects what most people who are head teachers or aspire to be head teachers believe in. The difference is that it's written down in black and white and in a concise format that you can refer to (Unit 2 commentary).

There are three important themes here:

1) The accessibility, specificity and concreteness of the standard.
2) The standard as affirmation of practice.
3) The aspirational aspect of the standard.

The first theme is significant because it allows learners to clarify expectations and provides clear guidance on action. However, there is a noticeable variation as to which element of the standard strikes a particular candidate as significant. For those who are new to management or who have not constructed what they do in a managerial framework, the functions often have the most impact. For others it is exploring values or looking more closely at their professional abilities they find most interesting.

The significance of the second theme is the need for affirmation that emerges strongly for both primary and secondary candidates. The standard allows them to make judgements about their performance and is seen as providing legitimacy for their actions that boosts their self-confidence. More practically the SHS serves as an external authority which provides them with a basis for making claims for opportunities, resources and permission to innovate within the school. In this sense it has three functions:

- Personal validation and hence positive emotional impact on the candidate.
- Political support in that it legitimates the candidate's position and actions.
- Resource procurement.

The third theme indicates the importance for candidates of the inclusion of a strong statement about professionalism in the key purpose and the professional values section of the SHS. This in part relates to theme two since it significantly adds to the authority of the standard if it is seen as having, or can be claimed to have, a moral authority within the profession and to embody for the candidates and their colleagues a 'respectable' vision of what they might want to become.

At a more pragmatic level, another major advantage of the standard, which also emerged in an earlier study of the use of management competences in the Strathclyde region (Reeves and Forde, 1994), is that it allows candidates to acquire a 'language' for describing and discussing management practice: 'It's given me a language to raise things, greater confidence, I articulate things much better, you can explain to yourself, recognising what I was trying to do, recognising what had gone wrong. I am more conscious, more aware, I can explain and articulate my ideas' (interviews).

This quotation contains an important element of aspiration embedded in the notion of entry into the 'discourse' of leadership and management and the sense of being empowered by this. In some ways this acquisition of the language is more profound than simply developing the capacity to understand the jargon. One major reason for emphasising the importance of training for headteachers on the part of policy-makers is to support the drive to modernise the public services through the adoption of a managerialist discourse and practice. Our evidence would seem to indicate that the SHS does help to achieve this.

However, the SQH does not always elicit significant change in candidates. A few students, for one reason or another, are driven by the need simply to 'play the game' without learning much as a result: 'I suppose I do. I document everything and keep all the paper. I wasn't very good at keeping evidence. I'd do it for my class, evidence of the children but not for management things I tended not to write enough down' (interview).

Indeed, in response to the question, 'Is there anything new that you do?' the candidate replied: 'I don't think so.' Another asserts all this is nothing new:

> I think that a lot of the decisions I made were made in the light of my experience as an assistant headteacher prior to starting the SQH. That's maybe not what you want to hear but it's what I think. My own experience tells me that if I had started SQH as an assistant headteacher with less experience in post it would probably have helped me get to answers quicker and made me broaden how I looked at things. But

because of the experience I have had as a manager in a school and the breadth of over 10 years before I started SQH – I mean I do reflect on my own practice, that's part and parcel of what I have always done (interview).

Looking at the minority of candidates who claim to have gained little from their participation in the course the theme of already having the necessary experience comes across most frequently. This lack of perceived novelty could possibly be even more prevalent as an issue when looking at standards for teaching as developmental tools. Certainly our evidence indicates that the SHS appears to be having more impact at primary level where the experience of, and identification with, being a school manager is more likely to be novel to candidates.

On the basis of this evidence, the positive characteristics of the SHS as a basis for development seem to be as follows:

- It gave an explicit framework that helped people to understand what was required of them and to make sense of the role of headship.
- It gave people access to a language and a structure for thinking about their work.
- It provided an opportunity for self-assessment that boosted people's self-confidence.
- It was important that the standard was seen as authoritative, morally respectable and effective both for the individual learners and in negotiation over access to suitable learning opportunities.
- The standard carried more impact when it clearly signalled new forms of development for the learner.

The place of reading

Whereas virtually all candidates go through the processes U1–U3 in order to be able to produce the portfolio, this is not the case with the commentary and the reading stages R1–R3, as outlined in Figure 7.2. In fact, in the initial evaluation of the programme, where many of the respondents were on the accelerated route and therefore claiming for prior learning, there was quite a strong resistance to using the literature (Morris and Reeves, 2000: 522) based on a rejection of the use of 'theory'. In part this signalled an ongoing struggle between the practical and the academic approach to teacher development in participants' minds.

This kind of resistance is less frequently expressed by standard

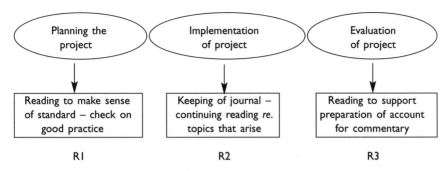

Figure 7.2   Preparing for the portfolio

route candidates but, nevertheless, the work they produce shows there is still probably an element of ambivalence about this aspect of the learning programme.

Most candidates will do some reading at R1 but this may be quite restricted and largely done to meet the terms of the assessment for Unit 1. Some, however, will use reading to guide their planning and to explore the options open to them in managing their project. These 'prospective' readers are more likely to continue through R1–R3 and the more sophisticated shaping of their account in the commentary often reflects the fruits of this process. A significant number of candidates will largely confine their reading to R3 and therefore use it retrospectively to shape their experience. This contrast is picked up by one of the candidates: 'At this point in Unit 2 I am now using/and know I am using the literature more to anticipate, plan my actions. However on a day to day basis it is the confirmatory way that is more commonly used' (Morris, 1999: 22).

For those who do continue with the reading, the major benefit they believe they derive is increased adaptability through the opening up of new options: 'having done some of the reading and the tutorials I was able to look at different ways of structuring things. That allowed me to sit and think about things before I went into them on instinct' (interview).

From the evidence of the commentaries, few candidates on Unit 2 went beyond a concern with technical and cultural issues at an operational or tactical level. Their reading is very much tied to questions relating to practice:

- Building self-confidence through affirming practice and beliefs.
- Preparing for action by checking out strategies and building knowledge.

- Investigating options.
- Seeking answers to particular problems (for example, delegation).

These are not traditional 'academic' concerns and only occasionally, where a candidate disagrees with a particular initiative or opposes a prevailing style of management, is there any apparent critical engagement with more fundamental issues of principle or the texts themselves.

For many, reading is used as a means of confirming they are on the right track and hence they are disinclined to question current orthodoxies. Texts are largely treated as authoritative: 'Own experience so far has been that the literature has been central to this reflective process – one measures oneself against the edicts/advice etc. in the best texts' (Morris, 1999: 22). One participant, however, did point out that these texts got rather tedious after a while.

What is interesting about the feedback on reading from the interviews is the primacy reading has as a source for both affirmation and new ideas. However there are limitations placed on the influence of reading because of candidates' concerns with practicalities and the need to put a stamp of legitimacy on their practice. For us this remains as a practical problem of delivery in that we regard it as essential that aspiring headteachers do have a wider view of their context in terms of understanding the background to the current state of the education service and the various tensions this reflects.

The key role of reading within the overall experience seems to have been as follows:

- Like the standard, it provided access to a language and a way of making sense of practice and experience.
- It was used in an affective sense to provide support for candidates' practice and to increase their self-confidence and self-esteem.
- It provided access to new ideas, gave people options for action and provided new ways of interpreting what was happening in school.

Self-evaluation

The importance of reflection on practice is generally recognised by SQH candidates, as one explained: 'Crucial – must constantly reflect on why we do things – who benefits. Looking at how we can provide young people with a better quality of education; a more personal and community experience – very relevant' (Morris, 1999: 22). Never-the-less, at a meeting of candidates at the end of the pilot there was some agreement that reflection was not, as one described it, 'part and parcel of what you do normally – you almost have to be taught, given permission to do it'. The SQH was seen as having had some success in giving this permission and encouraging reflection among candidates, as one argued in her response to the initial evaluation report:

> The SQH does make you reflect on what you are doing – it clarifies your weaknesses (e.g. delegation skills – my weakness!) and highlights your strengths. So far, main boon of SQH has been to remind me if used to reflect critically on one's own values and to re-establish them at the heart of one's practice (*ibid.*: 20).

For current candidates the process continues to be important. The external evaluators' survey in 2000 (Malcolm and Wilson) showed that 90 per cent of candidates said they were more reflective as a result of their involvement in the course. Examples of how this was perceived are contained in the interview responses: 'The critical log that I used was highly valuable. It was a tool for reflection. I would write things down, notes to myself and then used it for writing the critical commentary which was really valuable' (interview).

For some there is the danger of perhaps being over self-critical:

> So, yes, I did find it difficult. I think I maybe did find it difficult because I was analysing my performance or analysing how things worked out at the end of the day, whether it was successful, whether staff had moved on or whether how I had done it was enabling staff to move on. So maybe I found it difficult because I had been self critical because of the course. Maybe if I hadn't been on the course I wouldn't have been so self critical (interview).

The SQH creates an added pressure in requiring candidates to express and describe their professional selves and articulate what they think, believe and want to achieve in the commentary. This is often both difficult and 'embarrassing' for candidates: 'The most uncomfortable aspect of this course so far has been holding up for scrutiny my present practices and processes and the values that underpin them' (Unit 1 assignment).

An essential issue in such public reflection is how candidates situate themselves in this process. However, many candidates do recognise this is something that is worth overcoming: 'Values have tended however, to be implicit in projects and actions. Very real benefits arise through making these positions explicit from the outset. In future I would seek opportunities to articulate my values' (Unit 1 assignment).

In many ways the benefits of self-evaluation were usefully summarised by those candidates who were on the first pilot:

They felt validated by the experience.

It helped them identify areas for improvement, they found the professional abilities particularly useful in this respect.

It made them focus more on people skills.

It raised the importance of personal awareness of values and how these related to practice (Barry, 1999).

Support in the workplace

The evidence is this regard is equivocal in that the only data we have relate to the role of the supporter and were derived from the survey undertaken by Simpson *et al.* (2000). This tells us relatively little about the specifics of the interactions from the candidates' viewpoint. There is almost no comment in the interviews on the experience of network groups, tutorials or interaction with the supporter and, although there is more information referring to headteachers, this is still quite sparse.

When Simpson *et al.* surveyed the candidates in the summer of 2000, they found that just over 70 per cent of candidates regarded the role of the supporter as necessary, and these respondents felt the two most important functions the supporter served were as a sponsor:

Encouraged me to undertake the course
Makes it possible for me to carry out the work in school

And as a professional counsellor who:

Is a sounding board for ideas
Acts as a critical friend.

About a fifth of the sample did not think the supporter was particularly useful to them.

On the whole candidates were more likely to be satisfied with an internal supporter than they were with someone coming into the school from outside. Certainly the sponsoring role is probably more effectively managed by a powerful insider who also has the advantage of contextual knowledge when it comes to acting as a professional counsellor. An interesting issue in this regard is touched on in the following quotation, which makes very clear the level of 'supervision' that may be involved in having your headteacher as your supporter:

The one thing I found awkward was my headteacher sitting in as well. It's a difficult position to be doing all this work with her sitting there. She was very supportive but it was a pressure I put on myself. I kept trying to see things from her point of view, how she would have done it (interview).

Other social processes have already been touched on in the earlier part of the discussion, particularly the importance of the relationship between the candidate and other staff. Usually the staff most nearly concerned were members of a working party that had a responsibility for taking forward the particular priority which had been agreed as the objective for the candidate's project.

As the SQH is largely work based and requires the candidate to lead a whole-school initiative, enrolment on the course is usually a matter for public knowledge within the school. Candidates and their colleagues in school could be seen as engaging in an initiation process whereby the former enter a new role as 'aspiring headteachers'. Usually colleagues are seen as sympathetic:

> It has its drawbacks sometimes when I did put out things like questionnaires, especially in the PSD one, the staff one. The children were wonderful at it but the staff – I had to do it again because a lot of them ticked the boxes because they thought it would help me in my course. I had to get the message across to them that they were not helping anyone if they were not honest. They knew I was doing the PSD for the course. I didn't put out the questionnaire for the course but because it was part of my development in the school as well as doing the course. So I had to get the message across – 'Please be honest. It's nice of you to want to help me to pass this module but!' (interview).

The candidates' level of commitment to the course is likely to be substantially increased because they have voluntarily made a public and 'irrevocable' choice to join the course and accept the role. In order to maintain face there is a lot of pressure on them to succeed (Weick, 1995). One of the striking features of the SQH is the unusually high retention and completion rate for a work-based scheme.

Even where the group is less supportive the pressure to succeed remains very high. The guilt attached to doing something for your own career development can be used against some candidates. Several commentaries showed this was a real tension in a number of schools:

> In general the 'satellite group' had a good group atmosphere but there was always a feeling that this was 'my baby' and this was confirmed to me by a remark passed on not one, but several occasions by one of them, 'You have more at stake in this than us after all, it's your SQH project' (Unit 2 commentary).

This may also go to explain why securing benefits for the school is so important to candidates.

The other risk for many candidates lies in feeling obliged to challenge the status quo. There are two key themes that are remarked upon as being central to the SQH: staff participation and evaluation. It is somewhat surprising that these are seen as innovatory given how long both have been embodied in advice to schools (HMI, 1988; 1991). Nevertheless, the number of respondents who claim their schools do not normally use consultative procedures is high and evidence from the portfolios of accelerated route candidates also demonstrates the general weakness of evaluative procedures in schools. In cultural terms the course can therefore open up areas of tension within the school. Here is someone who feels they were trying to adopt a participative approach that ran counter to normal management practice in the school:

> In some respects I felt I was trying to work in two directions. I wanted the staff to see that I was sympathetic to their problems in developing writing. I also wanted to show the headteacher that I could take the staff with me and get positive results and feedback by the way I interacted with the staff (Unit 2 commentary).

The following is another case where the candidate recognises the importance of symbolic behaviour in more overt opposition to the prevailing ethos:

> I was excited and challenged by the project from the beginning. I had my own ideas about the way learning and teaching and people should be managed which were in conflict with many of the values of my school. I was already convinced that by setting up a more democratic culture I could develop a homework plan which would lead to improvement. My behaviour that day [INSET] gave the staff the opportunity to speak their mind and for their opinions to be considered. Had I been dismissive or judgemental the staff would have been reluctant to participate in the process of change. This meeting was vital in setting the tone for the change in school culture that I hoped to achieve (Unit 2 commentary).

This kind of challenge is less overt in the secondary texts although a theme in several of the accounts is the reordering of work because of the claim that a more strategic and holistic view of an initiative has been developed as a result of someone being on the SQH:

> More than for most developments I have undertaken, a good deal of time was spent on planning this project. This was partly because of the innovative nature of the approach within the school. A more well-worn approach to these tasks would have been to divide them up among the various members of the senior management team. In order to create some coherence of approach, it was important to ensure there was a coherent vision of what was to be attempted. It was certainly the case

that there was a major realignment of some tasks under my management (Unit 2 commentary).

What emerges from this discussion is that, in many ways, social processes serve both as sources of support and pressure, often at one and the same time:

- The importance of sponsorship and being given appropriate opportunities to learn and the obligation this places on the learner.
- The importance of personal support, particularly when confronting difficulties and problems.
- The risk and pressure involved in being publicly assigned important responsibilities and being seen as introducing new ways of working.
- The motivational value of working with a team of colleagues and the fact that any innovations are jointly tested and adopted.

The nature of learning

Knowledge and understanding of processes and context

Whilst we have already given a range of examples where candidates are claiming changes in their behaviours at a fairly general level, we also have examples of far more detailed accounts of the change process. A number of these indicate the development of understanding and knowledge over time as a result of the interaction between experience and reflection. The extract below is fairly typical. It is part of a longer account where there is a sustained concern both to gather and to respond to feedback during the process of change, which pushes the author to keep developing her practice and finding new ways of responding to the various capability issues the feedback highlights:

In drawing up the project plan my focus had been on determining and agreeing strategies for a consistent whole-school approach to the teaching of writing. The idea being that with concrete direction, teaching and learning in writing would improve and standards would be raised. I began however (as a result of my reading), to question my attitude about what I was hoping to achieve and how this could be done. By this stage, I had begun to realise teachers' understanding of the importance of writing as a process would have to be developed (Unit 2 commentary).

She then goes on to realise the continuing need to develop the meaning of 'writing' when classroom monitoring (the first stage of implementation) demonstrates that the teachers and herself need to discuss and explore further what they regard as quality in children's writing and the processes by which this is assessed and achieved. She concludes:

> The project itself will take much longer than originally anticipated to complete, but I believe taking time to develop the teachers, the agents of change in the classroom, will ensure that the policy when written will be successfully put into practice and this will be demonstrated in children's levels of achievement.

This is a fairly common feature of Unit 2 commentaries where an almost implicit theoretical stance is developed in the text focusing on key processes such as developing staff capability, increasing staff participation and improving communication and teamwork. What the most convincing work shows is the importance of maintaining an open and evaluative stance as a basis for shifting ideas and hence practice.

Continuing with the theme of reflection on externally generated data, in the following extract a change in practice is accounted for as the result of a different perception of context. This candidate claims to have moved from a very task-orientated approach to one where personal and cultural issues now influence his practice and have lead to a change in management style:

> There were various fault lines that impeded development: there was for instance, a division between the practical and the non-practical subjects which was exacerbated by splitting the school into two faculties along practical and non-practical lines. There was also a curious split along gender lines which saw the women on the staff being far more engaged with whole-school issues, while the men tended to get on with subject based developments. In this context, the staff review and development project was far more than just an opportunity to tinker with staff development procedures. It struck at the heart of the way we function as a staff and if it was to work we had to have the support of all the staff. I rejected the idea of using a working party to develop this project on the grounds that working parties, no matter how representative, only involve a fraction of the staff and therefore run the risk of being seen as partial (Unit 2 commentary).

This is linked to a set of insights about his own behaviour, described at a slightly later stage in his interview: 'Generally I haven't tended to be terribly consultative. The collegiate agenda of the SQH pushed me in the direction of consultation. It was time consuming but we did things properly, people were consulted and different views were taken into account'. He says he is now convinced this participatory approach is more effective and he contrasts the outcomes with a description of his previous practice that typifies what Creemer (1997) described as a 'project' school: 'I have had experiences over the years where bright new initiatives that I was convinced about and perhaps a minority of the staff were keen on, we launched them with great fanfares and they withered within a year or so' (interview).

This link between the external and the internal in terms of self is a very common feature of the accounts where being 'forced to act' in a different way pushes someone into confronting previous assumptions – a version of cognitive dissonance as presented here in the concluding section of a commentary:

> I am finding a balance, that mid-point between over- and under-management, between self-reliance and deputation. I continue to resist the temptation to bombard with memos, guidelines, rules and reminders, aiming instead for a clear comprehensive policy that is easily summarised and referred to. I have learned to adapt styles in areas such as evaluation where timeliness, honesty and accounts of key informants have become priorities rather than a one hundred percent response to a printed questionnaire. Alongside my desire to spur school 'partners' to action, has grown an awareness of the need to stimulate thinking: reflection. I suspect I am looking for a parallel movement to my own shift from strategic planning to strategic thinking (Unit 2 commentary).

In other cases the sense of personal impact is much lower and accounts present a more techno-rational basis for changing behaviour:

> Previously we treated review and evaluation rather briefly – some call it review and audit. I take a much more developed view of that nowadays than I did before. In the past the headteacher might give you a job to do, something from the Authority, and you just got on with it. You just tore into it. Now we are more likely to stand back and say, Why are we doing this? What is the evidence? I take that bit more seriously and the evaluation bit too (interview).

This was allied to a claim that there has been greater debate and discussion within the senior management team on these issues, partly as a direct result of involvement in the SQH which hints that argumentation and social processes may have been a key element of learning here as well.

Identity and power

Besides this more conventional form of learning associated with the development of knowledge and understanding of 'the world', there is also strong evidence of the importance of a change in the understanding of self and the perception of self-efficacy. A significant number of candidates from the primary sector highlighted issues of professional identity. Even people who had been in a senior post for some time, including those who are already headteachers, found composing the portfolio and commentary quite a powerful experience. Entry into the language, the discourse associated with the SHS, seems to function as a means of realigning and/or affirming a professional identity about which the person has maybe been unsure (Knowles, 1993). It is almost, for some candidates, as though they are redefining themselves through the process and affirming their identity as a school leader and manager:

> At this point I would state that the most important thing learned or achieved is for me to have begun to think like a manager and not solely as a teacher. The way in which I view matters and have approached the work which I have carried out over the course has changed dramatically as time has progressed (Unit 2 evaluation).

> It has completely changed my thinking. It has changed my abilities, my confidence. I am in an acting head post and I am thoroughly enjoying it – I don't think I could have coped with the difficult situation here without the SQH – I could have floundered (interview).

As we have already noted, what also comes through in these quotations is the link between a successful experience of the project and feelings associated with increased self-confidence and self-esteem. Some people also note an increase in their personal power in other ways as a result of their involvement in the programme: 'I maybe make him [my headteacher] stop and think every so often. There are maybe things I would say to the headteacher that I would not have said before – I have the language (interview).

Another candidate made the following observations:

> I also get the feeling from some of the heads round about that they are a wee bit scared of me now. A wee bit of insecurity about what we who have done the SQH have done that they haven't. I am a bit ahead of some of the others in things like evaluation. When the EO [education officer] talks about that you can see some of them looking at each other whereas I think, 'Yes, I know what I am about here' (interview).

What these quotations indicate is that there is an intermingling of two sets of responses: first, the adoption, or confirmation, of an identity as a school leader and manager; and, secondly, the power this identity and the knowledge on which it is based confer on the candidate. A triangular relationship is inferred between knowledge, power and identity and, for a number of candidates where these links are perceived as positive, this has reportedly had a dramatic effect on their capability and taste for action.

Accounting for change

Lastly it is important to consider certain key features of the accounting process in order to underline some of the key features of developing practice.

There are several common themes in the commentaries, one of which is the difficulty many candidates have with delegation, something they must successfully demonstrate in their portfolio. Below are three extracts where candidates explain why they feel they are now able to delegate effectively:

> Although I felt at the time that I spent the day catching precious minutes to keep abreast of the work, in hindsight it was much better that I had to delegate it fully. I learned through clear instructions and the careful choice of personnel work can be delegated with no worries. I also feel there is a greater sense of staff ownership now, than if I had been present (Unit 2 commentary).

> However this year I have reflected much more on the amount of work that I perform within the group. The tension between teaching staff volunteering and requiring tasks to be completed by definite times has caused me to take on more than is realistic. This project has made me analyse people's motivation for being involved. I have realised that by developing a system of motivation through personal and professional development that groups can progress themselves. Leading by example is important but I realise in leading if you want to be trusted you must trust others (Unit 2 commentary).

> In general, I feel that sometimes I sacrifice my sense of humour, when I feel under pressure to get certain work done, and I need to give attention to this. However, I feel I have more confidence about trusting that a team will take forward tasks and policy developments. They have developed their vision and their evaluative systems so that my direct and detailed role is much less (Unit 2 commentary).

These extracts illustrate how individual and personal the process of changing practice is. Delegation is not an abstract idea for these people; it is woven into personal perception through a unique mixture of associations bound up in a particular context. Each of these candidates claims to have arrived at the same insight about the value of delegation and some commonality about the means to achieve it but by their own individual route.

Conclusions

One of the most striking things about SQH candidates' accounts of learning that has changed their practice is the very personal and situated nature of their explanations of change. These do not reflect the rather technical-rational and abstract descriptions that are often given of the practice of critical reflection but point to a rather more visceral process where the personal and the professional are very closely intertwined. They also indicate the crucial role of the social arena in which change occurs and the importance of the micro-political dimensions of changing practice.

By pulling together the summaries about the efficacy of the various elements from each theme in our first section, the experience of learning, the reader can draw some conclusions about the value of combining features from each of the three models of WBL we outlined in Chapter 5.

What we feel emerges from the data is that a focus on a developmental model of performance management can be both rigorous and effective. The points we would want to emphasise reflect the importance of some of the features our respondents identified:

- Self-evaluation.
- An evidential focus on action in context; an openess to feedback; frameworks for interpretation and analysis that include an examination of values and assumptions; a shared language.
- The social context for learning and the affective aspects of change; moral authority, aspirational respectability of goals, level of challenge; collegiality and shared responsibility for organisational goals and outcomes; sense of agency, self-esteem and personal control.

These are features that need to be given very serious consideration in formulating and implementing any policy for performance management, and they indicate that successful improvement of professional practice involves much more than the introduction of a simple management technique to enhance individual accountability.

8

Assessing performance

Introduction

In the previous chapter we explored what it means to undertake a substantial programme of work-based learning (WBL) by looking at the experiences of participants pursuing the Scottish Qualification for Headship (SQH) programme. A clear sense of the power of WBL emerged from this exploration and the contribution of the assessment system to learning was touched upon. In this chapter we want to look at assessment in greater detail because assessing performance in a valid and reliable way that supports individual development is not straightforward.

We need to consider how to design and implement an assessment process that examines the quality of the performance and outcomes achieved by the participant completing a WBL programme. In order to do so we need to address a number of questions:

- How should performance be defined, and what aspects of it should be assessed?
- How do you gather evidence about performance?
- How do you ensure the assessment tasks support improvement in the learners' practice rather than distracting them?
- How do you balance the need for rigour and validity against the need for practicality?

To address these questions we will reflect upon some of the issues that arose in the development of the assessment framework for the SQH programme and during subsequent research into the submissions produced by candidates completing the WBL units.

Background

Whilst we will be concentrating particularly on the role of assessment in work-based learning and therefore the processes we have used for assessing Units 2 and 3 of the SQH programme, it will be helpful to the reader to have some overview of the assessment framework for all four units as a background to the discussion.

The overall framework (see Table 8.1) was designed to make sure that the terms of the SHS are fully met by the time the candidate completes the whole programme. Unit 1 concentrates on self-assessment against the three elements of the standard and the planning of the learning programme for the candidate for Unit 2. Units 2 and 3 are concerned with achieving competence in relation to the four key management functions, including addressing issues of values and purpose and demonstrating the ability to apply and learn from the use of the techniques of critical reflection. Unit 4 concentrates on enabling candidates to form a more holistic overview of the role of school leadership. Candidates are required to prepare a report on the outcomes of having undertaken a comparative study of leadership and management practice in another organisation in either industry, commerce or a different public service. In addition their strategic understanding is examined through being interviewed about their approach to school improvement in their current setting and their response to a critical incident.

There is also an accelerated route for experienced senior managers where the assessment framework differs in that these candidates prepare a portfolio of evidence and a commentary covering all four man-

Table 8.1   The framework of assessment for the SQH programme

Unit title	Mode	Assignments
Unit 1 The Standard for Headship	Taught	Self-assessment report and project and learning plans
Unit 2 Managing Core Operations (Learning and Teaching and People)	WBL	Portfolio and commentary
Unit 3 Managing School Improvement (Policy and Planning, Resources and Finance)	WBL	Portfolio and commentary
Unit 4 School Leadership	Taught	Comparative study report and final interviews

agement functions based on their prior experience. In effect they make a claim for accreditation of their prior experiential learning. The assessment of Unit 1 differs in that the candidates do not submit project and learning plans but the assessment for Unit 4 is exactly the same as for those on the standard route.

Issues in assessing performance

Is assessment necessary?

If we are to achieve our ambitions to use structured professional development in the workplace as the means of improving performance, we need to consider carefully the nature of the assessment process. Assessment, when limited to notions of 'testing', is a bolt-on extra designed to ensure candidates have acquired the learning objectives specified for a particular programme. Such a model of assessment divides learning from the assessment process. However, assessment can be integrated into the learning process and can provide a structure for the programme to secure opportunities for candidates to undertake, reflect on and evaluate in some depth their practice in school. Assessment also has other benefits, such as establishing structured opportunities to review performance, providing formative as well as summative feedback and giving the public recognition necessary for teachers facing increasing demands for accountability regarding both their practice and their ongoing development. Finally, assessment can be part of quality assurance, ensuring the achievement of an acceptable standard that is critical in a programme that links personal and organisational development. However, to achieve these benefits we need to establish an appropriate balance between assessment as a legitimate part of the development process in WBL and as a realistic guarantee of a standard of performance, which still leaves the question of what we mean by performance and how can we practically assess its quality.

Defining performance

The move to WBL has meant that the privileging of knowledge and understanding in traditional assessment schemes for academic awards has been replaced by an emphasis on a range of outcomes related to performance specified as competences. However, the move to competence-based assessment has been severely criticised largely because it is argued that the emphasis on skills has led to an assessment process that is behaviourist in terms of both the focus and the unit of assessment (Barnett, 1994). Indeed a common method in early competence-based programmes was to focus on the functions required for a job and to specify the associated behaviours in order to develop clarity about what was being assessed. Under this regime the learner's task is to provide evidence that each particular skill has been undertaken. However this mapping of the completion of sub-units can lead to fragmentation in which the skills or minor components of skills are assessed in isolation – on a 'can/cannot do' basis. The learning programme can become driven by assessment with the learner focusing on gathering specific items of evidence to prove the completion of each discrete skill rather than improving practice through engaging in a coherent learning programme.

An alternative approach was adopted in the SQH programme in which the assessment framework and process are based upon the Standard for Headship (SHS). It is worth recalling briefly the construction of the SHS because of its pivotal role in the assessment process. The SHS embeds management functions into a wider map of school leadership and management, combining them with professional values, knowledge and understanding and professional abilities, which include both interpersonal and intellectual abilities (see Figure 6.2 on page 104). These various elements are integrated through the key purpose of headship which is 'to provide the leadership and management which enables a school to give every pupil high quality education and which promotes the highest possible standards of achievement' (SOEID, 1998a: 4). In the SHS the definition of competence links all three elements:

> Competence in relation to the Standard for Headship is defined as the ability to combine these three elements appropriately in practice. Thus, in order to be judged competent an aspiring headteacher must show that s/he is capable of achieving the key purpose by carrying out the key functions of headship, drawing on appropriate professional values and abilities (*ibid*.: 3).

If candidates are to be judged competent they must demonstrate they can achieve the key purpose of headship. Implicit in this definition is the idea that the candidate must be successful. One of the first issues we had to deal with in the development of assessment for the WBL units in the SQH programme was this issue of 'success'.

The meaning of success

In some schemes of experiential learning it is possible for a learner to undertake a practical project that was unsuccessful but that still proved to be an extremely important personal learning experience. For example, a participant trials a new thinking skills programme but, because of the lack of differentiated materials to meet the range of needs in the class, the achievement of learning outcomes is limited. In these circumstances the learner can make the most of these negative experiences in his or her analysis by examining ways of differentiating the programme more effectively. Although the experience may have been negative or limited, the quality of the critical appraisal of that experience can indicate significant learning has taken place. Indeed, it could be suggested that an insistence on 'success' limits opportunities for creativity and risk-taking because learners will operate within limits of safety rather than trying to alter their practice fundamentally.

In the SQH programme, however, an overarching criterion demands that learners must undertake the school-based project successfully and demonstrate improvement as a result of their work. In schemes such as this, given the scale of the projects, there are limits to the degree of experimentation and failure that are tolerable in a whole-school setting. If organisations are to improve and serve the needs of the pupils better, then staff development as a major improvement tool has to be more clearly focused on supporting effective practice, and any assessment process has to demand a standard of performance. Making critical reflection on an unsuccessful work-based project acceptable detracts from the idea that structured and assessed programmes of staff development can improve current practice rather than simply 'inform' future good practice.

Although we are stressing the primacy of 'success' as a criterion in the assessment process, we are not suggesting there is a clear and definitive standard of success to be applied universally across different contexts. It has to be accepted that the degree of success is variable. As we noted in Chapter 6, schools and other organisations differ dramatically in their capacity and capability for improvement. Thus 'success' will necessarily be different in different contexts. A simple example of this difference would be the contrast between the outcomes achieved by two learners seeking to develop and enhance participative structures. In one school where there has been a long-standing schism between departments, the establishment of a cross-department working group with a functional level of operation will be regarded as a successful outcome. In contrasting circumstances, in a school where mixed teams are the norm, success will be in terms of the enhancement of this process, for example, by delegating successfully to the team a major element of the development work. These two contrasting examples demonstrate the importance of setting outcomes and success criteria for the work-based projects that reflect the specific context in which they are to be implemented whilst at the same time conforming to good practice as described in the competence framework.

The emphasis on success does raise questions of equity, especially for those candidates working in difficult circumstances where their opportunities to develop skills and to demonstrate their ability to achieve successful outcomes are limited because of the circumstances in the school. Limited management processes to support school development, an overly bureaucratic culture, narrow remits, staff resistance and limited leadership in the school are some of the features that learners can do very little to change but which can have a major impact on their progress. What can constitute an objective proof of performance when the success of an individual candidate's performance rests on other people in the organisation behaving in certain ways? We have to ensure the assessment processes used are fair and equitable as well as valid and reliable.

Designing an assessment programme

As Broadfoot (1996: 141) notes, the increased attention to professional development has altered approaches to assessment: 'It is in the area of professional learning in particular that there has been a recognised need to engage learners with developing the full range of professional skills and a rapid realisation of the value of new approaches to assessment'.

Side by side with this are the significant changes, noted by Mitchell (1989: 60) , that accompanied the development of standards where there has been a move away from testing individuals with regard to specific traits to 'a consideration of a more legalistic notion [which] relies on the collection of evidence of suitable quality for reasonable inferences of an individual's competences to be made'. This idea of assessment being essentially about gathering and then judging evidence is vital in the design of WBL. The school has to be the place where evidence is gathered because the focus is on the learner's performance in that context. However, assessment in the workplace can never completely cover all aspects of practice and, therefore, we need to consider what methods can be used to gather sufficient evidence to provide a holistic view of an individual's performance and what the parameters should be for judging evidence in relation to candidates' contexts for action.

Further issues this evidence-based process raises are those of ownership and confidentiality. Using realia as evidence means the consent, involvement and level of exposure of people other than the learner in the assessment process must be governed by a clear and agreed code of conduct.

There are broadly three ways in which we can gather evidence about performance: by observing performance, from the learner's and other's accounts of their performance and by gathering evidence about the impact of performance. We will consider how useful each of these is a means of assessment.

Developing an approach to assessment in the SQH

One obvious option for the assessment of performance is the use of observation. Assessment by observation may include techniques such as shadowing, planned observation and simulations. In shadowing the learner is accompanied by the assessor through day-to-day work, dealing with activities as they arise naturally in the workplace. In planned observation, preset activities are observed, again in the workplace. However, both methods can sample only practice and may miss vital aspects of performance. An alternative is to design simulated tasks where specific aspects of performance will occur. In simulations, which usually are conducted outside the workplace, participants are observed as they complete set tasks either individually or working as a member of a group.

The above techniques might, on the face of it, seem the most likely method of assessing performance. However, if performance is based upon the expanded notion of competence we apply within the SQH programme, there are difficulties in using observation as the primary method of assessment. In observational assessment there is the tendency to take snapshots of distinct items of behaviour. In the field of school management events such as meetings, interviews or presentations are easy to observe. Similarly in teaching, didactic sessions are easy to identify. Focusing on areas such as these emphasises certain aspects of formal management or teaching and neglects others, such as ongoing relationships, handling the long-term elements of strategy and progressing the complete management or learning process over time. Examining performance more holistically requires lengthy observations to produce sufficient and relevant information related to the elements being assessed and it is questionable how truly representative these observations would be. A more fundamental criticism relates to the construction of professional development. Self-evaluation and critical reflection drive learning in the SQH. To base assessment primarily on the observation of specific aspects of behaviour by another person ignores these elements and does not allow opportunities for the learner to make sense of his or her own performance. Where observation is used it must be accompanied by lengthy debriefing sessions to enable participants to reflect upon, to evaluate and to make sense of their own performance.

For the WBL units in the SQH programme we needed to find a method of assessment that covered all three elements of the standard. Given the limitations of observation we needed to consider other methods of gathering evidence through the accounts of performance by learners and through examining the artefacts generated in the course of, and as a result of, their actions.

These two approaches can be combined to provide a powerful means of assessing WBL. However, there are a number of issues that needed to be considered. The preparation of an account of performance is a demanding task and there is a danger the learner's focus will be on producing the account rather than undertaking the tasks. There is the additional danger that the judgements will focus predominantly on how well the learner has put together the account rather than what was actually achieved in school. Gathering evidence about the course and impact of performance also raises questions about contextual differences: what is a major breakthrough in one school will be everyday practice in another. There are also issues relating to the question of sources. Should only the staff be involved or pupils also? Should views from other stakeholders be sought, such as parents, local agencies, members of school boards or governing bodies? Though this range of respondents could provide insight into various aspects of the participant's work there are some practical considerations. The form and scale of the feedback need to be manageable but, further, the wider the pool of respondents the greater the care that has to be taken not only in relation to the handling of evidence confidentially but also in judging the reliability of the evidence being presented.

Assessing the WBL units

In a development programme predating the SQH, the Management Competences Scheme, we used a combined 'portfolio' that included items of evidence to illustrate the conduct of a project related to a specific key function and a commentary reflecting critically on the project. However, as Reeves and Forde (1994) noted, there was a tendency in the commentary for learners to be descriptive, usually outlining the events of the project and relating these to specific items of evidence rather than critically reflecting upon the process of management and on their own development.

In the SQH programme, therefore, we decided to separate the portfolio of evidence from the commentary and present these as two separate but interdependent tasks. The portfolio provides evidence of the process and outcomes of the practical project against the relevant key functions in the SHS. The commentary is an extended critical reflection (between 5,000 and 6,000 words) relating the practical project back to values and purposes. The intention behind this division was, first, to enable learners to provide sufficient detail about the project to support a valid judgement of performance and, secondly, to stand back and consider their experience holistically by relating it to ideas gained from reading and discussion in order to demonstrate the fulfilment of Element 1 in the SHS (the professional values). However, there was a danger that separating the portfolio and the commentary would devalue the portfolio by reducing it simply to a file of papers illustrating discrete and minor tasks that were not related to the wider purposes. Further, the commentary could become a discussion of principles with little reference to the candidate's own practice and experience. From our analysis of the submissions (Forde *et al.*, 2000; Reeves *et al.*, forthcoming) we have found that the portfolio and the commentary are capable of supporting the development and assessment of performance. We will examine the role of each of these assignments in turn.

Portfolios and commentaries: examining connected practice

Portfolios

In the SQH the portfolio should contain the following:

- A guide to the construction and layout of the portfolio and the links between different elements.
- Claims for competence for each of the core activities (the sub-units of the management functions) that relate specific aspects of the project to the relevant sections of SHS.
- Different kinds of evidence linked to specific core activities, including evidence of their work and the impact of this on the performance of others and on the development of the school.
- A statement by the headteacher verifying the contents of the portfolio.

The basis for the assessment of the portfolio is the set of criteria that has already been used for planning their learning by the participants and this is one of the reasons why this helps to make these portfolios a powerful learning tool. In the portfolio the participant is required to:

- test actions against purposes;
- develop a holistic view of management process; and
- evaluate his or her performance in terms of the outcomes achieved.

The portfolio is the framework in which the actions the participant took to sustain the development and achieve the set outcomes are analysed and presented.

A sample of portfolios judged to be 'good' by assessors was analysed in terms of the overall structure, the content of the claims for competence and the patterns in presenting evidence. This analysis shows that the portfolio could be a very powerful learning and assessment tool by requiring the learners to make connections between different aspects of their practice.

In the SQH it is the SHS that provides the scaffolding for the learners to analyse their practice and to demonstrate the process they undertook to achieve a successful outcome within a specific social context. This analysis begins with the learner, first, constructing 'the story' of the project and, secondly, by examining the project from different perspectives in order to compose claims for competence that relate the relevant parts of the story to the core activities of management specified in the SHS. Below is an example of the first stage, where the candidate develops the story of her project on improving the environmental studies (ES) curriculum in a primary school:

- Worried about provision in ES, agree as a staff to put it in School Development Plan;
- Worked with staff to audit current programme and identified areas not covered;
- Working group put forward new topics to ensure broad, balanced, progressive and coherent programme from P1–P7;
- Worked out mapping in terms of knowledge, understanding and skills for each stage to cover needs of all learners;
- Staff teams wrote forward plans based on these structures; discussed, agreed and shared with all staff who used them;
- Monitored forward plans, teacher's evaluations and pupils' work;
- Developed system for staff to do their own auditing of learning;
- Identified needed better assessment procedures to track progress – teachers having difficulty with this;

- Organised staff INSET day on assessment in ES;
- Arranged time so that staff worked in teams on end of topic and skill based assessment units.
- Monitored results, teacher's evaluations, pupils' work.

The story maps out the broad steps and phases of the project from which the learner can then identify the relevant aspects of the story that relate to specific core activities within each management function. We can illustrate this by exploring an example of a claim for competence for Core Activity 2.1.1, which is: 'Develop structures for the management and evaluation of effective learning and teaching'. This encompasses the following three tasks:

(a) Develop and implement effective structures for curriculum planning to ensure breadth, balance, progression and coherence in the school's curriculum that meet the needs of learners.
(b) Plan and maintain systems to ensure effective implementation of programmes of study and assessment procedures ensuring that the learning needs of all are met.
(c) Agree, develop and implement systems to monitor, evaluate and improve learning and teaching programmes (SOEID, 1998a: 7).

Below is a claim for competence relating relevant parts of the project on environmental studies to Core Activity, 2.1.1. Composing a claim for competence enables the learner to reconstruct the management process as it was conducted in a particular setting:

> The project on the review and development of the school's Environmental Studies curriculum demonstrates my competence in developing structures for the management and evaluation of effective learning and teaching. The project began with a curriculum audit of current provision. I drew up a draft questionnaire to identify current topics taught at each stage including science and health and distributed it to all staff from P 1 to Primary 7. I worked with the working group to analyse the results of the audit and identify areas from the 5–14 curriculum document not covered. I then set the working group the task of developing several new topics which would ensure a broad, balanced, progressive and coherent programme from P1–P7. Once a draft of this had been discussed with the whole staff I worked with the group to map each topic in terms of knowledge, understanding and skills for each stage to cover needs of all learners. In term two stage partners wrote forward plans based on these structures and implemented the topic over that term. A major task for me was to monitor this work by looking at forward plans in Environmental Studies to ensure all the areas were being covered at each stage, pupils' work on displays, pupils'

portfolios and I collaborated in group teaching on developing investigative skills. I also devised, distributed and collated a questionnaire for the teachers' evaluations of the topic they delivered. I used monitoring evidence to write a brief evaluation report for the SMT.

In this claim for competence, we see the participant exemplifying 'process knowledge' (Eraut, 1994) in a specific area of practice.

Characteristically in claims for competence the details of the context and the purposes of the project or activity are set out and, sometimes, the project is justified in terms of school needs. Details of what the candidate did are set out in sequence from planning to implementation to the outcomes achieved. The outcomes reported tend to be the immediate results of a task rather than a more strategic view of overall outcomes. However, these immediate results are used to point to a level of success. Alongside these outcomes are evaluatory comments used frequently in relation to choice of strategy or conduct of the task. Finally, although learners are making claims for their own competence, the notion of collaboration is still central to the process of the project and references to 'I' are balanced with references to 'we', 'the staff' or 'the group'.

The same project can cover a number of core activities across different functions. Thus this project on environmental studies was used by the learner to claim competence for an aspect of managing people (that is, Core Activity 2.2.2: 'Develop teams and individuals to enhance their performance and that of the school' – SOEID, 1998a: 7). In the claim for competence below, the candidate makes sense of both the project and the nature of school management by relating aspects of the project to this core activity. In this claim, references to specific items of evidence are also included:

A significant element of the project on Environmental Studies was the staff development programme with provision for both the whole staff and individual teachers. The key strategy was a programme of school based staff development which I planned and delivered collaboratively with other members of the working group. My first task was the identification of the development needs of the staff. I used the results of the audit to produce a short questionnaire [3a 'Collated questionnaire'] identifying areas for the Inset programme from which I drew up a draft programme [3b 'Draft of programme'] and circulated this for comment to all staff. There were some minor changes to the proposed programme but practical work and investigative skills was an area that needed to be addressed. Here I adopted two strategies (1) I arranged for two members of the working group to attend a local authority inservice course on planning a balanced Environmental Studies programme

(2) I arranged that the two other members of the group visit another school [3c 'INSET programme'] nearby to look at investigative skills in science. We used the material gathered during these two activities to create Inset workshops [3d 'Group's notes for workshops']. Then all staff were set the task of planning with their stage partner using the new format. I conducted an evaluation of the inset programme and it was judged to be very useful [3e 'Collated evaluation']. The second phase of the staff development was class based support for which I met with each pair to plan collaborative teaching. At the end of the third term I asked the staff to review and evaluate the progress of the project and this indicated that the staff development programme had enabled staff to implement specific units developing investigative skills in their class successfully [3f 'Evaluation of programme'].

Initially, the issue of evidence – what and how much – was a thorny one for us. Some portfolios were very large and the quality of evidence was variable. Participants reported frustration in having to develop lengthy submissions and the assessors reported that judging the material was very time consuming and that much of it was irrelevant in that it did nothing to represent a process. Increasingly we are emphasising the need for an action-orientated and 'peopled' approach to selection that clearly demonstrates crucial stages in the process showing what the candidate did and how others responded. Evidence that charts the progress and the impact of the project, including monitoring and evaluation material, is particularly useful. This material can come from a range of stakeholders such as staff, parents, pupils and other groups who have either been involved in the project or affected by the outcomes. In addition indirect evidence can be included, particularly witness testimonies from those involved or effected by the outcomes of the project. However, by itself the portfolio is an inadequate test of the SHS. Therefore the portfolio is complemented by the commentary.

Reflecting on purposes and practice: the commentaries

The commentary is the vehicle for assessing candidates' commitment to educational values, their commitment to their own learning and continuous professional development and their knowledge and understanding of school leadership and management. The commentary is intended to act as a medium for supporting cognitive development in which candidates reflect critically on their role and performance in the practical project drawing on literature to consider, in the light of their experience, the key principles that should underpin their practice. As we can see from Table 8.2, the commentary has an equally strong link with practice as the portfolio.

This is demonstrated in the extract below, where the learner looks back over the project she has led on introducing monitoring to the school to map out the key principles underpinning successful practice in this area:

> The need for monitoring to be embedded in the development cycle of the school has been constantly reinforced for me through the implementation of this project. It is essential that it is accepted by staff and implemented through an ongoing process. In any evaluation exercise we have to know what we are measuring – there has to be specific criteria that will tell us whether we are successful or not and a systematic way of gathering information. We also must have ways of developing those aspects which are found to be lacking and take appropriate action to ensure these are corrected. Where success is evident we must analyse why this is the case and use the information in future developments. All the information has to be shared with the relevant personnel to ensure a shared understanding and commitment to any change necessary. This may lead to development of new criteria for success and so the cycle continues. Bush and West-Burnham (1994) quotes Aspin *et al.* (1992) '. . . evaluation needs to be seen as an integral part of the management process . . . it must be a continuous subject of attention and must be soundly embedded in the structure and culture of the organisation. If it is a stage in the process it can be put off; if it is integral to the process it cannot'.

It might be argued the learner is simply reiterating theoretical principles that could be drawn from any standard text. However, it is clear

Table 8.2 Reconstructing and reflecting on practice

Aspect	Portfolio	Commentary
Purpose	To map out sequence of actions and outcomes against the relevant key functions in the standard	To examine critically issues and themes that emerged from relevant key functions
Analysis	Claims for competence relating specific tasks and evidence to core activities	Exploration of critical issues or episodes in conduct of project
Evaluation	Evaluation of project and evidence to illustrate outcomes achieved	Evaluation of approaches against purposes and intentions

these ideas have been drawn from very powerful learning experiences that now underpin the actions and decisions taken by the candidate, both on a day-today basis and strategically in relation to this area of management. It is not simply the acquisition of a body of knowledge that is facilitated and tested through the commentary. Values and purposes also come across strongly in this extract.

The lengthy analysis and reflection demanded by the commentary provide an opportunity for the learner to get inside the school-based project and to explore not just the process and the outcomes but to test specific strategies and approaches against values and purposes. The commentary, as we can see from the next extract, is also an opportunity to reflect upon some of the more difficult issues faced by practitioners in school and to relate these back to the purposes underpinning practice:

> The most overt purpose of the Teaching and Learning project was to create a structure for more effective delivery of teaching. However, I intended any change of structure to mark changes in attitude in the classroom and to force review of courses as they were revised to fit the new shape of delivery. So on the surface the working group were simply looking at the blocks of time which were allocated to subjects; when those blocks of time should be scheduled and which subjects should be set against each other in the timetabling blocking. Important as these matters were they were never reviewed in isolation but as a starting point to a more thorough going review of the first and second courses with the ultimate aim of helping to raise achievement. In the course of the session it became apparent that the two projects which I had undertaken, the Teaching and Learning Review and Professional Development and Review Project were much more closely inter linked than I had realised at the outset. The main purpose of the professional development and review project had initially been to develop a system of monitoring and evaluation that would support staff in their development planning and also ensure quality assurance. As my reading made me more aware of the importance of underlying values, I started to realise that, by promoting the notion of self evaluation and review of classroom teaching, this project was travelling in the same direction as the curriculum review project: to raise pupil achievement.

In Chapter 4 we talked about linking the personal schema (the learners' personal values and their views and feelings about themselves as practitioners) with the procedural schema (the skills aspect of practice combined with the contextual considerations in pursuing a specific course of action) and the theoretical schema (the principles and concepts underpinning practice). We can see how these different aspects come together in the final extract from a commentary:

> Establishing the cultural transformation and ensuring all staff had a stake in the new plan, was done through consultation and communication. My methods of consultation and communication varied as the project developed. From past experience within the school communication was not always seen as a two-way exchange but merely as directive. Staff have been unhappy in the past with both lack of communication about new developments and lack of opportunity to give their views. As suggested by Colin Riches (Bush and West-Burnham, 1994, P254) 'Mistakes are often made because communication is not seen as a two way exchange, but as directive from above, without consideration for whom the communication is intended, or of their views'. In order to create the correct psychological conditions to motivate staff and to make effective, long-lasting improvements to the school I was committed to using participative management styles. I wanted everyone on the staff, and not exclusively the working group, to feel they had a stake and a say in the change of policy that would be taking place. This required a cultural transformation to ensure the whole staff had the ability and confidence to make choices, to solve problems and to be fully involved in implementing, monitoring and evaluating the homework plan. My task was not only to communicate with the staff but also to create opportunities for them to give their opinions on the way things were or should develop. I tried to achieve this by using a variety of methods of communicating with the staff. I felt too many formal meetings, too many formal memos, audits or feedback sheets would demotivate staff rather than enthuse them and that they may begin to dread the words 'Literacy Plan'. I used a combination of staff meetings, informal discussions with the members of the literacy working group, staff audit and feedback sheets, informal and formal staff memos and the parent information evening to consult and communicate with the whole staff.

In this passage the personal comes strongly through the learner's description and judgements about his own performance and about the values upon which he has based his practice: 'I wanted everyone on the staff and not exclusively the working group to feel they had a stake.' These ideas combine with the technical/procedural issues ('I used a combination of staff meetings') which are then set within the cultural context of the school: 'Staff have been unhappy in the past both because of lack of communication about new developments.' However, the context is not used as the only justification for adopting a particular approach. What is clear from the next sentence is that this approach is derived from theoretical understanding: 'this required cultural transformation to ensure that the whole staff had the ability and confidence to make choices.'

For the WBL elements of the SQH programme we have tried to develop assessment methods that make conceptual interconnections, and this is the power of the portfolio of evidence and the critical commentary. The portfolio acts as an organiser of procedural knowledge by building links between the technical, the contextual and the personal schema. The commentary acts as an organiser of theoretical knowledge by building links across the personal, the technical and the contextual schema with the theoretical dimension.

In Chapter 5 we outlined how self-analysis, analysis of practice and principles and theory could be linked together powerfully in WBL. Figure 8.1 takes that model and indicates how the portfolio and commentary can be seen to fit together into this cycle and used as the basis for assessing this learning process.

Tensions and dilemmas

One of the most persistent problems in devising any system of assessment is balancing the need for rigour and reliability against the

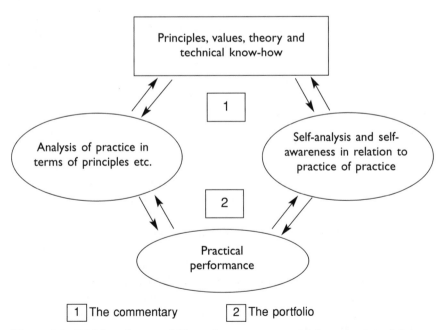

Figure 8.1 Linking the portfolio and commentary to the conceptual framework for practice

developmental benefits of the process. In assessing performance too much emphasis on the former tends to lead to an onerous emphasis on satisfying ever more detailed criteria to the detriment of worthwhile learning. Another facet of this dilemma is the balance within the assessment process among self-assessment, assessment by others within the school and the involvement of the employer and external agencies in the process.

Field assessors

By relying on the account of performance prepared by the participant it might be argued it is the participant's judgement upon which the assessment is based rather than on the quality of the performance. We are right to be cautious about the validity of assessment if we rely solely on these accounts to assess performance. It is important to emphasise in the SQH programme that the portfolio is not simply a presentation of 'what might or should have been' but is grounded in the actual practice that occurred. The portfolio is a public document that depicts what happened and is verified, first, by the headteacher and, secondly, through the field visit to the school. An agenda for the field visit is drawn up collaboratively by the tutor and field assessor after each has assessed the written submission. The agenda is then sent to the school to be distributed to those involved: the headteacher, a colleague involved in the development project and the participant. The main aims of the field visit are to verify the contents of the portfolio and to seek clarification for any areas or aspects that are not fully covered in the submission.

One of the underpinning principles of the SQH is combining theoretical and practitioner perspectives. The use of the field assessor from a practice background – either a headteacher or a local authority adviser – to make a school visit is an important way of maintaining this link. Field assessors have credibility in the field derived from their own experience, which they can draw on in making judgements concerning the performance of the individual candidates.

The field visit is seen as a way of accessing the perceptions of others in the school about the candidate's work. This, however, has sometimes been more problematic than we anticipated, for a number of reasons. It has been important to emphasise that the visit is solely concerned with the performance of the individual candidate and not the whole school, particularly where there are concerns related to the quality of the work undertaken by the candidate. In a collaborative culture it is desirable that staff are mutually supportive. However, there is a danger that only bland responses are given by interviewees which give no real indication of the quality of the individual learner's work. This can be partly overcome by probing from the field assessor but, in some cases, it is difficult to extricate the performance of the individual from the work context and the factors that may have supported or prevented him or her performing appropriately. Reading the micro-politics of the school environment therefore becomes a critical aspect of the field visit.

Assessing interpersonal abilities

The assessment of professional abilities, particularly interpersonal abilities, is seen as a crucial in the assessment of performance for school managers. These abilities are difficult to assess using a portfolio because they are rarely evident in material evidence. In the SQH this area is explored during the field visit but even so we are conscious we are relying on reports of performance from a very limited group of respondents.

The list of interpersonal abilities in the SHS is formidable but it is intended candidates use these to become more aware of their characteristic modes of behaviour and use their strengths to compensate for areas where they feel less secure. Again self-evaluation has to be at the heart of this process. However, making this kind of judgement about yourself without feedback is very difficult.

A method used in many organisations is a 360-degree survey in which a range of colleagues and clients provide feedback on the performance of a manager. We have adapted this process for use at the end of the Unit 2 project to provide formative feedback to candidates so they can identify development needs they need to address in the course of Unit 3. At the end of Unit 3 the evidence from a second 360-degree survey is used as a part of the summative assessment of that unit.

Retrospective claims

Whilst this discussion has been confined to the assessment of candidates on the standard route of the SQH programme it is worth while contrasting candidates' experience of this process with that of those candidates who are making claims for prior experiential learning on the accelerated route of the SQH programme. The latter do not undertake work-based projects. Instead they assemble evidence drawn from their activities prior to joining the course to make claims for competence. As a learning process preparing this type of portfolio and commentary is far less satisfactory and satisfying both for the candidates and for the school in terms of having a positive impact on practice. Frequently, candidates are having to try to engage in activities that can be used to evaluate processes and outcomes 'after the horse has bolted', which is far from ideal. There is a sense, for a number of participants, in which they feel they are having to impose 'a story' on their past that does not ring true and that the portfolio exercise feels like a matter of jumping through hoops.

Accreditation

With a national qualification such as the SQH it is essential a robust system is in place to ensure both the quality of delivery and the standard of the learning outcomes achieved by successful candidates.

Accreditation provides important benefits both for the individual learner as well as for the employing organisation and the wider educational system. For the individual learner this public recognition is important, especially in terms of advancement in career, although the beneficial impact of achieving an award in terms of self-confidence and improved self-esteem should not be discounted.

For a national service, having a basis for establishing parity in the standards achieved in professional qualifications is desirable. Accreditation can help to ensure provision is made within the terms of an established quality-assurance procedure that would be difficult to develop and implement within a small organisation, and that there is a sound basis for establishing parity of professional qualifications nationally.

The recognition of the importance of process knowledge (Eraut, 1994) in professional practice has led to a range of developments in higher education: experiential programmes, WBL and learning contracts (Boud and Solomon, 2001). As a consequence we were able to validate the SQH programme under the quality-assurance procedures applying to postgraduate awards.

Of course we also should not lose sight of the fact that accreditation of WBL has had important benefits for the higher education sector in Scotland. Its development has given rise to significant developments in creating alternative methods of delivery and assessment at the same time as enhancing the higher education institute's role and contribution to the continuing professional development of teachers.

Structural implications

The other essential area for consideration concerns the aspects of assessment that are linked directly with the issues we raised in Chapter 7 about the structures required to support learning. It took us over five years of piloting and readjustment to develop our assessment instruments. All the assessors on the SQH programme, whether they are field or tutor assessors, undergo three days of training in addition to being expected to attend joint moderation meetings. This level of investment in equipping people to undertake the tasks involved has been and remains crucial to the quality and credibility of the assessment process. We would want to emphasise the importance of assessors having the skills and understanding required to undertake this sort of exercise if they, and those whose work they are assessing, are to have confidence in its credibility.

We also deliberately chose, having investigated the separation of assessment and training in the original version of the National Professional Qualification for Headship, to adopt a system that ensured assessment and professional development were directly linked. This linkage is made both through the emphasis on self-assessment and by linking assessment by others into the learning support system and we remain convinced this is crucial in supporting improvement.

Finally, we have pointed to the importance of context in terms of assessing work-based learning which entails that negotiation and agreement take place prior to learners' engagement in the learning process so they know exactly how the criteria for assessment will be interpreted in their particular context.

Conclusions

If performance management is about the improvement of practice, our experience would suggest there are a number of key issues in using assessment as a productive process in this regard.

First, we would emphasise the importance of self-evaluation as part of the improvement process. Roger (1999: 124) observes that, whilst we are generally given to taking a positive view of our own performance: 'Where individuals are asked to assess their performance in relation to different aspects of their job rather than to compare themselves against other employees, evidence suggests that they are more discriminating in their judgements than their managers and that their assessments are also realistic and "objective".' So whilst self-evaluation is no guarantee of accuracy, given the right circumstances, it is likely to be more accurate and detailed than the judgement of others. However, this does not touch on the major advantage of self-evaluation, which is that learners are much more likely to respond actively to needs they have identified and understood for themselves than to those needs others try to convince them of.

Secondly, what is assessed needs to be carefully considered. Outcomes alone are not sufficient and neither is the exploration of performance as simply a matter of skills: values and purposes are equally important. Preferably, assessment should be in terms of meaningful professional processes rather than being simply focused on an isolated piece of practice divorced from its context. The assessment process and its outcomes need to be meaningful to practitioners if they are going to find them useful and productive.

Thirdly, if assessment is not actively part of a learning process and linked into future action, it has far less impact on practice. A retrospective focus is not very motivating even when the assessment is positive. The contrast we have found between the responses of candidates on the accelerated route and those on the standard route underlines the need for any assessment and feedback to be timely and to have an immediate currency for learners as part of an ongoing endeavour to develop their practice.

Fourthly, assessment, where it is done by others, needs to be credible, professionally respectful, serious, and fair, which means that the context for action has to form part of the basis for making judgements.

9

Achieving improvement: developing policy and practice in schools

There is no doubt that change within schools and across the education service is vital if we are to improve practice and achieve each child's right to an education suitable for his or her needs. The demand on schools to improve their performance in a context where the judgement of the quality of the education service is linked directly to the economic and social well-being of the country can prompt a search for 'a quick fix': some means of demonstrating immediately improvement to a political audience and popular audience alike. Nevertheless, any assumption that performance management, through the mechanism of appraisal and the engagement of individuals in continuing professional development (CPD), will provide 'an answer' to the need for reform in schools is unlikely. Certainly there is little in the experience of various initiatives over the past 25 years to suggest this will be the case. Equally, the hopes of the modernisers that dramatic change will come about when the old bureaucratic values that imbued the public service disappear are probably wishful thinking. Michael Barber's (1999: 207) analogy that teachers, like the Welsh miners, will be swept away as a result of their resistance to change is unlikely to occur in the near future. The ability to benefit from managerial models predicated on 'down sizing' or globe hopping to the most exploitable environment and being able, as a result, to threaten to fire your employees into either compliance or oblivion is equally unlikely.

As a result the need to engage *with* teachers in bringing about reform will be unavoidable in the end. Under these circumstances adopting a long-term and principled approach to the issue of enhancing performance seems to us to be the best way forward. Schools need to establish for themselves exactly what they wish to achieve and select and modify procedures and structures accordingly.

There is also a need before embarking on any course of action to acknowledge what we do not know. Certainly there is little hard evidence that current approaches in education are sufficiently effective to support improvement across the whole system. Whilst there are techniques (outlined in Chapters 3 and 5) that are likely to have positive effects on some aspects of practice, particularly when teachers are being inducted into the profession, there is a great deal we do not know about how experienced practitioners improve their performance. We know relatively little about the impact of CPD on practice or the operation of particular approaches such as the use of critical reflection and action research. Nor is the evidence from industry on the effectiveness of performance management techniques as clear cut as some would have us believe. Popular models for improving organisational performance such total quality management (TQM) – drawn from the practice of exemplary Japanese enterprises – have proved far harder to transplant to other contexts than their advocates expected. Notions such as 'the learning organisation', whilst attractive, tend to become rather opaque when it comes to working out who exactly is learning what and how the resulting knowledge is embedded and used in the organisation. The number of detailed empirical studies into the processes underlying change and improvement in practice is small, whereas the number of exhortatory texts in this area is huge.

The other crucial parameter to bear in mind is the nature of the change in practice that is being looked for. We believe this to be quite fundamental and central to defining teacher identity. In many ways the key assumptions that underpinned teachers' practice in the past are now materially altered. Some of the major strands in this change in Scotland are:

- *Social inclusion* In the past schools were about selecting and educating to a high standard a minority of the school population. This has dramatically altered over the last ten years and, for many teachers the change in focus requires a substantial alteration in attitudes as well as the acquisition of new skills.

- *Relationships* There is a fundamental shift in the relationship between learners and teachers formally marked by such initiatives as the United Nations Rights of the Child. The basis for engaging learners in the education process is changing and, again, this has important implications for teacher identity.
- *Learning* The nature and purpose of learning are undergoing a major revision both in the light of a growth in the understanding

of learning processes and in the change in capabilities young people need to acquire. The growing access to knowledge has profound implications for the role of the teacher and undermines the old transmission model and the basis for much of the current curriculum.

- *Boundaries of professionalism*   Teachers are being asked to work in new ways – for example, as part of multi-professional teams in new community schools or to engage in fields such as health promotion they have traditionally seen as falling within another professional sphere. All teachers are now expected to engage in the management and running of their schools and to accept a personal professional responsibility for their schools' functioning rather than simply being concerned about their own classrooms.

Taken together these trends amount to a profound alteration in the underlying psychological contract for teachers. Changing one's practice to operate effectively within these parameters implies far more than the acquisition of a few new skills. The largely content-based programmes of staff development that accompany major initiatives in schools are inadequate to address this task. Current provision, where the main focus is to develop sufficient knowledge and understanding and skill in relation to the individual staff member receiving the development (such as the early literacy and numeracy initiatives), will not address these fundamental issues. Teachers will need opportunities to engage in understanding the implications of these changes and exploring the means of responding effectively to them through a consistent, persistent and progressive action-orientated approach to professional development.

Our belief is that the kind of changes required of the education service cannot be achieved purely through the use of an individualised approach to performance management. Without a better understanding of the complexities of professional learning we would argue that current strategies are highly unlikely to yield the kind of results presaged by the wording in central government policy documents.

The focus on the individual teacher contained in these documents shows a lack of recognition of the strength of the social context in shaping a teacher's ability and willingness to pursue change and improvement. Any strategy for improvement, we would argue, must be based on an understanding of teacher learning within the social context of the school.

Putting learning first

The danger in adopting a simplistic approach to performance management is that, whilst motivation is clearly an essential element in maintaining and enhancing performance, it is not sufficient as the basis for the more substantive forms of improvement required under current circumstances. Whilst there are strengths to be found in the managerial model, for instance, there is no doubt that greater clarity about expectations can have important benefits as illustrated through the impact of the Standard for Headship in the Scottish Qualification for Headship (SQH) programme. However, such specifications can only form part of any approach and they carry with them a number of dangers in a situation where there is a need to explore new forms of practice. Learning has to be the key objective. We need to reconstruct our understanding of CPD through radically rethinking the fundamental principles that should underpin provision and improving our knowledge of the learning processes involved in practitioner's learning. Instead of being largely concerned with the content of what is delivered, we need to pay far greater attention the provision of an environment that supports teachers' learning, first, by putting learning processes at the centre of our planning and, secondly, by putting these processes at the centre of the core purpose of the school.

We would therefore like to encourage headteachers and their staffs to adopt a fairly radical approach to improving performance. Rather than simply adopting technical elements of the various models we feel it is more worth while to concentrate on the process of professional learning and use what is known about this as the basis for guiding practice within their schools. A key issue here is that of action. If learning is not actively located in practice, it is unlikely to be effective. It is the learning of teachers in action that makes a difference to their behaviour and therefore the task of performance management is to explore the ways in which such learning can be supported in school and how external provision and networking with other institutions can best enhance that support. In that exploration we also believe there is a need to move away from seeing learning purely as a rational process located within individuals to looking at it as a socio-political process embedded in the school community that impinges on teachers' professional identity and self-esteem.

For the individual there needs to be public acknowledgement and support for his or her role as a learner, whether it is as an aspirant manager or as a teacher seeking to improve his or her practice. The role of learner needs to be legitimated within the profession. In order to achieve this, opportunities for development need to be firmly linked to action, supported and resourced; they need to have the backing of the headteacher and local authority and be regarded as worthwhile by participants and their colleagues. Learning can then become part of the discourse of the school: learning is out in the open, forms a basis for the discussion of practice and is, in turn, subject to evaluation in action. Learning in these circumstances is visible in terms of the performance of both individuals and groups and performance is shaped by and in turn influences the social climate in which this learning occurs.

Another essential element in ensuring the public legitimacy of this learning is agreeing that what is to be achieved is desirable. The goals of any professional development programme for individuals must be seen as consonant with professional values so that engagement and success confers an increase in social capital and ensures learners feel motivated and challenged to effect the desired improvement in practice.

Importantly, learners should also be in charge of shaping their own learning by making transparent what their practice is, why it is justified and how its purposes are best achieved. It is in this that some element of prescription in the form of standards, competence frameworks or benchmarks has its use in providing learners with a schema for action that can then be translated by them into the context of their school. Paradoxically, the power of such a framework is not in its specificity but in a looseness of definition that promotes discussion among its users and its adaptability to the specifics of a particular context. It is important that criteria derived from standards are similarly flexible enough to allow for experiment and creativity. What a standard or a competency framework can provide is the means for practitioners to plan, review and judge their performance and to take charge of their own learning.

Managing to enhance performance

The structural implications of seeing the school as a major site for teacher learning are significant. Supplying teachers and their supporters with the tools and the skills for learning means serious consideration has to be given to developing capability to provide the environment and skills for this approach to CPD.

Lessons from launching the SQH underline the need to develop the capability of the school as an organisation to support the adoption of a professional development approach to performance management.

We need to think further about the nature of the school as an organisation that exists for the purpose of fostering learning – both for pupils and teachers - and create a congruence of structure, culture and processes in the pursuit of that goal. Teacher learning cannot be constructed as a process that occurs outside the school, for example, on a training course run by the local authority or academic programme in a local university. Instead we need to reconstruct teacher learning by situating it within the 'community of practice' the school represents. Work-based learning provides the means by which teachers grapple with real issues that relate to the aims and purposes of the particular school and, at the same time, the major issue of their own professional/social identity within that context. Learning that will bring about significant change in practice will bring about change not only in skills and understanding but change in the way in which a learner sees him or herself and is seen, in turn, by others within the community in order that improvements in practice can be achieved.

The systems in the school and the local education service need to be deliberately designed to counter those aspects of the environment that militate against learning. This means we need to consider not only accommodating both pupil learning and teacher learning within the same institution but the cross-fertilisation of these two areas of activity. The increasing emphasis in relation to pupil learning on balancing the cognitive with the affective and social domains is vital. Learning to learn has become the keynote of school curricula. A similar approach has to be developed to teacher learning.

We need to counter isolation of individual teachers trying to develop and improve their practice by actively building a community of practice through establishing systems for mentoring, coaching, peer observation and other opportunities for interaction. Setting up systems to allow interaction and encourage debate about what constitutes good practice, what should be the way ahead, is vital and something in which teachers and potentially pupils can be involved. Opportunities for interaction and debate need to be enriched with access to ideas from outside the organisation. A key part of building up capability is to consider the channels for introducing and disseminating new information and ideas as well as improving internal communication to spread and communicate ideas in-house.

Building capability should be concerned not only with establishing structures but also with increasing the capacity of all members of the organisation to learn how to learn. Earlier we commented on the importance of not just providing opportunities for learning but valuing these tangibly by providing tools and resources and by culturally making learning public and legitimate. Side by side with this we need to ensure people have the capability to learn from work-based programmes by enabling them to develop the skills of planning, evaluating and reflecting critically on their own practice.

If we are to improve performance we need seriously to undertake the process of increasing capability and capacity to deliver the ideal of a learning profession not only within individual schools but also across local authorities and providers, particularly higher education institutions.

Engagement and professionalism

Earlier we commented on the limitations of change initiatives based on prescribing (in narrow terms) 'good practice' to be implemented by all without due regard to questions about the local context. There is a more fundamental reason why we should be wary of prescriptive approaches to bringing about change. We need to resist the current moves towards conceiving teachers as technicians simply delivering a set curriculum in the prescribed manner. Such a position not only disenfranchises teachers from engaging in consideration of purposes and aims but also carries the danger that we are left relying on teachers who are incapable of thinking about the purposes and context for education with deleterious effects for students and schools and ultimately for the education service. A well disciplined force inured to following and obeying the management will, like Marks and Spencer's employees, be left high and dry when the terms of the game suddenly get switched on them.

Prescription is dangerous because it is often reductive, implying the overall purposes of education are straightforward and easily obtainable. This position robs teachers of their professionalism. Here, however, we are not seeking to reinstate some nostalgic construction of professionalism in which individual teachers are trusted to exercise their own judgement without due regard to the legitimate expectations of others. Instead we are conceiving professionalism as the engagement of practitioners in the educative community in which they work as teachers and in the wider educational world. Teachers need to be part of constructing the future by debating purposes and aims alongside developing strategies to bring about improvement in specific areas of practice.

Making teaching attractive involves a massive re-engagement with a set of purposes for education people find worthwhile and admirable. If you cannot secure commitment to something people feel is intrinsically worth aspiring to then you are wasting your time trying to create ever more elaborate 'magical' performance management castles in the air.

1

References

Ackoff, R.L. (1980) The systems revolution. In M. Lockett, and R. Spear (eds.) *Organisations as Systems*. Milton Keynes: Open University Press.

Ainscow, M., Hopkins, D., Southworth, G. and West, M. (1994) *Creating the Conditions for School Improvement*. London: David Fulton.

Anderson, E.M. and Shannon, A.L. (1995) Toward a conceptualisation of mentoring. In T. Kerry, and A.S. Mayes (eds.) *Issues in Mentoring*. London: Routledge.

Apple, M.W. and Beane, J.A. (eds.) (1998) *Democratic Schools: Lessons from the Chalk Face*. Buckingham: Open University Press.

Argyris, C. and Schon, D. (1974) *Theory in Practice: Increasing Professional Effectiveness*. San Francisco, CA: Jossey-Bass.

Armstrong, M. and Baron, A. (1998) *Performance Management: The New Realities*. London: CIPD.

Baguley, P. (1994) *Improving Organisational Performance: A Handbook for Managers*. London: McGraw-Hill.

Ball, S.J. (1999) Labour, learning and the economy: a policy sociology perspective. *The Cambridge Journal of Education* 29(2): 195–206.

Barber, M. (1999) *The Learning Game; Argument for an Education Revolution*. London: Indigo.

Barber, M. and Phillips, V. (2000) Fusion: how to unleash irreversible change. Paper presented at the EAZ conference, Birmingham, Easter.

Barber, M. and Sebba, J. (1999) Reflections on progress towards a world class education system. *Cambridge Journal of Education* 29(2): 183–94.

Barnett, R. (1994) *The Limits of Competence: Knowledge, Higher Education and Society*. Buckingham: SRHE and Open University Press.

Barry, P. (1999) The professional development of prospective headteachers: a competence based approach. M Ed thesis, University of Newcastle.

Bayne-Jardine, C. and Holly, P. (eds.) (1994) *Developing Quality Schools*. Lewes: Falmer Press.

Bottery, M. (2000) *Education, Policy and Ethics*. London: Continuum.

Boud, D. and Feletti, G.I. (eds.) (1997) *The Challenge of Problem-Based Learning*

(2nd edn). London: Kogan Page.

Boud, D. and Solomon, N. (eds.) (2001) *Work-based Learning: A New Higher Education*. Buckingham: Open University Press.

Bourdieu, P. (1977) *Outline of a Theory of Practice*. Cambridge: Cambridge University Press.

Bourner, T., Bowden, R. and Laing, S. (2000) The adoption of professional doctorates in English universities: why here? Why now? Paper presented at the 3rd Biennial International Conference, Doctoral Education and Professional Practice: 'The Next Generation', University of New England, September.

Bradley, H., Conner, C. and Southworth, G. (eds.) (1994) *Developing Teachers Developing Schools: Making Inset Effective for the School*. London: David Fulton.

Broadfoot, P. (1996) Liberating the learner through assessment. In G. Claxton *et al.* (eds.) *Liberating the Learner: Lessons for Professional Development in Education*. London and New York: Routledge.

Brookover, W.B., Schweitzer, J.H., Schneider, J.M., Beady, C., Flood, P. and Weisenbaker, J.M. (1978) Elementary school climate and school achievement. *American Educational Research Journal* 15(2): 301–18.

Bruner, J.S. (1966) *Toward a Theory of Instruction*. Cambridge, MA: Harvard University Press.

Buckley, J. (1985) *The Training of Secondary Teachers in Western Europe*. Windsor: Council of Europe/NFER.

Burr, V. (1995) *An Introduction to Social Constructionism*. London: Routledge.

Bush, T. and West-Burnham, J. (eds.) (1994) *The Principles of Educational Management*. London: Longman.

Caldwell, B.J. and Spinks, J.M. (1988) *The Self-Managing School*. Lewes: Falmer Press.

Carr, W. and Kemmis, S. (1990) *Becoming Critical: Education, Knowledge and Action Research*. London: Falmer Press.

Chartered Teacher Partnership (2001) Website: www.ctprogrammescotland.org.uk

Clarke, J. and Newman, J. (1997) *The Managerial State*. London: Sage.

Cooper, C.L. and Locke, E.A. (eds.) (2000) *Industrial and Organisational Psychology*. London: Blackwell Business.

Cray, D. and Mallory, R. (1998) *Making Sense of Managing Culture*. London: International Business Press.

Creemer, B. (1997) Towards a theory of educational effectiveness. In A. Harris *et al.* (eds.) *Organisational Effectiveness and Improvement in Education*. Buckingham: Open University Press.

Dadds, M. (1994) Bridging the gap: using the school-based project to link award-bearing INSET to school development. In H. Bradley *et al.* (eds.) *Developing Teachers Developing Schools: Making Inset Effective for the School*. London: David Fulton.

Deming, W.E. (1982) *Out of the Crisis: Quality, Productivity and Competitive Position*. Cambridge, MA: Cambridge: University Press.

DES (1972) *Teacher Education and Training* (James Report). London: HMSO.

DES (1985) *Better Schools*. London: HMSO (Cmd 9469).

DES (1986) *Circular 6/86*. London: HMSO.

DETR (1997) *The 12 Principles of Best Value*. London: DETR.

Dewey, J. (1938) *Logic: The Theory of Enquiry*. New York: Henry Holt and Co.

DfEE (1997) *Excellence in Schools*. London: HMSO.

DfEE (1998) *Teachers Meeting the Challenge of Change* (green paper). London: HMSO.

DfEE (2000a) *Performance Management in Schools: Performance Management Framework*. London: DfEE.

DfEE (2000b) *Performance Management in Schools: Guidance*. London: DfEE.

DfEE (2000c) *Professional Development Supporting Teaching and Learning*. London: DfEE.

DfEE (2001) *CPD Strategy for Teaching and Learning*. London: DfEE.

DfEE (2001a) *Schools: Building on Success*. London: DfEE.

DfEE (2001b) *A Strategy for Professional Development*. London: DfEE.

Draper, J., Fraser, H. and Taylor, W. (1993) 'Assessing Probationers': An Opportunity for Professional Development. Edinburgh: Moray House Institute of Education, Heriot-Watt University.

Drucker, P. (1954) *The Practice of Management*. New York: Harper & Row.

Drummond, M.J. and McLaughlin, C. (1994) Teaching and learning: the fourth dimension. In H. Bradley *et al.* (eds.) *Developing Teachers Developing Schools: Making INSET Effective for the School*. London: David Fulton.

Duignan, P. and MacPherson, J. (1992) *Educative Leadership: A Practical Theory for Administrators and Managers*. London: Falmer Press.

Edwards, D. (1997) *Discourse and Cognition*. London: Sage.

Elkjaer, B. (1999) In search of a social learning theory. In M. Easterby-Smith *et al.* (eds.) *Organisational Learning: Developments in Theory and Practice*. London: Sage.

Eraut, M. (1994) *Developing Professional Knowledge and Competence*. London: Falmer Press.

Esp, D. (1993) *Competences for School Managers*. London: Kogan Page.

Evans, L. (1999) *Managing to Motivate: A Guide for School Leaders*. London: Cassell.

Fielding, M. (1999) target setting, policy pathology and student perspective: learning to labour in new times. *Cambridge Journal of Education* 29(2): 277–87.

Flood, P.C. (1998) Is HRM dead? What will happen to HRM when traditional methods are gone? In P.R. Sparrow and M. Marchington (eds.) *Human Resource Management: The New Agenda*. London: Financial Times/Pitman Publishing.

Forde, C. (1998) *The Management Competences Scheme: Interim Evaluation of Pilot Project*. Glasgow: St Andrew's College.

Forde, C., Reeves, J. and Morris, B. (2000) Are portfolios worthwhile: reflecting upon the evidence of the Scottish Qualification for Headship programme. Paper presented at the *European Conference on Educational Research*,

20–23 September, University of Edinburgh.

Freedman, P. (1998) The getting of wisdom? Consuming management education. Paper presented at the Higher Education Close Up Conference, 6–8 July, University of Central Lancashire, Preston (www.leeds.ac.uk/documents).

Fullan, M. (1991) *The New Meaning of Educational Change* (2nd edn). London: Cassell.

Gewirtz, S., Ball, S.J. and Bowe, R. (1995) *Markets, Choice and Equity in Education*. Buckingham: Open University Press.

Glover, D. and Law, S. (1996) *Managing Professional Development in Education*. London: Kogan Page.

Goddard, I. and Emerson, C. (1997) *Appraisal and your School*. Oxford: Heinemann.

Goodlad, J.I. (1979) *A Study of Schooling*. Bloomington, IN: Phi Delta Kappa.

Grace, G. (1995) *School Leadership: Beyond Education Management: An Essay in Policy Scholarship*. London: Falmer Press.

Griseri, P. (1998) *Managing Values: Ethical Change in Organisations*. London: Macmillan Business.

GTC (2001) *A Professional Learning Framework*. London: GTC for England.

Hagger, H. (1997) Enabling student teachers to gain access to the professional craft knowledge of experienced teachers. In D. McIntyre (ed.) *Teacher Education Research in a New Context: The Oxford Internship Scheme*. London: Paul Chapman.

Hamilton, R. (1993) *Mentoring: A Practical Guide to Mentoring*. London: David Fulton.

Hannon, V. (1999) On the receiving end: New Labour and the LEAs. *The Cambridge Journal of Education* 29(2): 207–17.

Hargreaves, D. (1996) *Teaching as a Research-based Profession: Possibilities and Prospects*. London: Teacher Training Agency.

Hargreaves, D. and Hopkins, D. (1989) *School Development Planning*. London: HMSO.

Hargreaves, D. and Hopkins, D. (1991) *The Empowered School: The Management and Practice of Development Planning*. London: Cassell.

Hartley, D. (1997) *Re-schooling Society*. London: Falmer Press.

Hatch, M.J. (1997) *Organisation Theory: Modern, Symbolic, and Postmodern Perspectives*. Oxford: Oxford University Press.

HMI (1988) *Effective Secondary Schools*. Edinburgh: HMSO.

HMI (1991) *MER 5: The Role of Development Plans in Managing School Effectiveness*. Edinburgh: HMSO.

HMI (1996) *The Annual Report of Her Majesty's Chief Inspector of Schools, Standards and Quality in Education 1997*. London. The Stationery Office.

HMSO (1991) *Citizen's Charter* (white paper). London: HMSO.

Holly, P. and Southworth, G. (1989) *The Developing School*. Lewes: Falmer Press.

Hopkins, D. (1987) *Improving the Quality of Schooling*. Lewes: Falmer Press.

Hopkins, D., West, M. and Ainscow, M. (1996) *Improving the Quality of*

Education for All: Progress and Challenge. London: David Fulton.

Hoyle, E. and John, P. (1995) *Professional Knowledge and Professional Practice*. London and New York: Cassell.

Huberman, M. (1993) *The Lives of Teachers*. London: Cassell.

Industry in Education (2000) *Milestone or Millstone? Performance Management in Schools: Reflection on the Experiences of Industry*. Industry in Education (industryineduc@hotmail.com).

Joyce, B., Calhoun, E. and Hopkins, D. (1999) *The New Structure of School Improvement*. Buckingham: Open University Press.

Joyce, B. and Showers, B. (1988) *Student Achievement through Staff Development*. London: Longman.

Juran, J.M. (1989) *Juran on Leadership for Quality*. New York: Macmillan.

Kainan, A. (1994) *The Staffroom: Observing the Professional Culture of Teachers*. Aldershot: Avebury.

Kelley, C. (1998) The Kentucky School-Based Performance Award program: school-level effects. *Educational Policy* 12(3): 305–24.

Kelley, C., Odden, A., Milanowski, A. and Heneman, H. (2000) *The Motivational Effects of School Based Performance Awards*. Policy Brief Consortium for Policy Research in Education. University of Pennsylvania.

Kerchner, C.T. and Elwell, C.L. (2000) Paying mindworkers: what is the incentive to teach? Paper presented at the Council for Greater Philadelphia Teacher Accountability conference, May.

Knowles, J.G. (1993) Life history accounts as mirrors: a practical avenue for the conceptualisation of reflection. In J. Calderhead and P. Gates (eds.) *Conceptualising Reflection in Teacher Development*. London: Falmer Press.

Kolb, D.A. (1984) *Experiential Learning: Experience as a Source of Learning and Development*. Englewood Cliffs, NJ: Prentice-Hall.

Konrad, J. (1998) Skill and competence needs of small and medium enterprises (SMEs) and for the creation of new companies (www.leeds.ac.uk/documents).

Labour Party (1997) *Labour Party Manifesto*. London: Labour Party.

Lave, J. and Wenger, E. (1991) *Situated Learning: Legitimate Peripheral Participation*. Cambridge: Cambridge University Press.

Leithwood, K., Begley, P.T. and Cousins, J.B. (1992) *Developing Expert Leadership for Future Schools*. London: Falmer Press.

Levin, B. and Riffel, J.A. (1997) *Schools and the Changing World: Struggling Toward the Future*. London: Falmer Press.

Lewin, K. (1952) Group decision and social change. On G.E. Swanson *et al.* (eds.) *Readings in Social Psychology*. New York: Holt.

Locke, E.A. (1997) Motivation through conscious goal setting. *Applied and Preventive Psychology* 5: 117–24.

Lortie, D.C. (1975) *School-Teacher: A Sociological Study*. Chicago, IL: University of Chicago Press.

Lomax, P (ed.) (1990) *Managing Staff Development in Schools: An Action-Research Approach. BERA Dialogues* 3. Clevedon: Multilingual Matters.

MacIntyre, D. (ed.) (1997) *Teacher Education Research in a New Context: The*

Oxford Internship Scheme. London: Paul Chapman.

Mahony, P. and Hextall, I. (2000) *Reconstructing Teaching: Standards, Performance and Accountability*. London: RoutledgeFalmer.

Malcolm, H. and Wilson, V. (2000) *The Price of Quality: An Evaluation of the Costs of the SQH Programme*. Edinburgh: Scottish Council for Research in Education.

Marker, W.B. (2000) The professional development of teachers. In T.G.K. Bryce and W.M. Humes (eds.) *Scottish Education*. Edinburgh: Edinburgh University Press.

Marris, P. (1986) *Loss and Change* (2nd edn). London: Routledge.

Maslow, A. (1954) *Motivation and Personality*. New York: Harper.

McMahon, A. (1996) Learning to become a headteacher. In G. Claxton *et al.* (eds.) *Liberating the Learner: Lesson for Professional Development in Education*. London and New York: Routledge.

McMahon, A., Bolam, R., Abbott, R. and Holly, P. (1984) *Guidelines for Review and Internal Development in Schools: Secondary School Handbook*. York: Longman for the Schools Council.

Mitchell, L. (1989) The definition of standards and their assessment. In J.W. Burke (ed.) *Competency Based Education and Training*. Lewes: Falmer Press.

Montgomery, D. and Hadfield, N. (1989) *Practical Teacher Appraisal*. London: Kogan Page.

MORI (1995) *Survey of Continuing Professional Development*. London: MORI.

Morris, B. (1999) *An Evaluation of the First Year of the SQH Pilot*. Stirling: Institute of Education, University of Stirling.

Morris, B. and Reeves, J. (2000) Implementing the National Qualification for Headship in Scotland: critical reflection. *Journal of In-Service Education* 26(3): 517–31.

Mortimore, P., Sammons, P., Stoll, L., Lewis, D. and Ecob, R. (1988) *School Matters: The Junior Years*. Wells: Open Books.

NCITT (1979) *The Future of Inservice Training in Scotland*. Edinburgh: SED.

NCITT (1984a) *The Development of the Three-Tier Structure of Award-bearing Courses*. Edinburgh: SED.

NCITT (1984b) *Arrangements for the Staff Development of Teachers*. Edinburgh: SED.

Nias, J. (1988) What it means to 'feel like a teacher': the subjective reality of primary school teaching. In J. Ozga (ed.) *Schoolwork: Approaches to the Labour Process of Teaching*. Milton Keynes: Open University Press.

Nixon, J., Martin, J., McKeown, P. and Ranson, S. (1996) *Encouraging Learning: Towards a Theory of the Learning School*. Buckingham: Open University Press.

O'Brien, J. (1995) The continuing professional development of teachers in Scotland. In J. O'Brien (ed.) *Current Changes and Challenges in European Teacher Education: Scotland*. Bruxelles: Moray House Institute of Education, Professional Development Centre, in association with the COMPARE-TE European Network.

Odden, A. (2000) New and better forms of teacher compensation are possible. *Phi Delta Kappan* January: 361–66.

Odden, A. and Kelly, C. (1997) *Paying Teachers for What They Know and Do: New and Smarter Compensation Strategies to Improve Schools*. Thousand Oaks, CA: Corwin Press.

OfSTED (1993) *Handbook of Inspection of Schools*. London: OfSTED.

Parker, M. (1998) *Ethics and Organisations*. London: Sage.

Peters, T. and Waterman, R. (1982) *In Search of Excellence: Lessons from America's Best Run Companies*. New York: Harper & Row.

Piaget, J. (1954) *The Construction of Reality in the Child*. London: Routledge & Kegan Paul.

Potter, J. and Wetherall, M. (1987) *Discourse and Social Psychology: Beyond Attitudes and Behaviour*. London: Sage.

Reeves, J. (1999) Development planning: tracking the complexities of change in Scottish schools. PhD dissertation, University of Strathclyde.

Reeves, J. and Forde, C. (1994) Can management competences support the development of a learning organisation? In *Proceedings of the Scottish Educational Research Association*, September, University of Dundee.

Reeves, J., Forde, C., Casteel, V. and Lynas, R. (1998) Developing a model of practice: designing a framework for the professional development of school leaders and managers. *School Leadership and Management* 18(2): 185–96.

Reeves, J., Morris, B., Forde, C. and Turner, E. (forthcoming) Exploring the impact of CPD on practice in the context of the Scottish Qualification for Headship (SQH). *Journal of In-Service Education*.

Reyes, P. (ed.) (1990) *Teachers and their Workplace: Commitment, Performance and Productivity*. Newbury Park, CA: Sage.

Roger, A. and Hartley, D. (eds.) (1990) *Curriculum and Assessment in Scotland: A Policy for the 90's*. Edinburgh: Scottish Academic Press.

Roger, S (1999) *Performance Management in Local Government: the Route to Best Value*. London: Financial Times/Pitman.

Rogers, C. (1983) *Freedom to Learn for the 80's*. Columbus, OH: Charles E. Merrill.

Rosenholtz, S. (1989) *Teachers' Workplace: The Social Organisation of Schools*. New York: Longman.

Rutter, M., Maughan, B., Mortimore, P. and Ouston, J. (1979) *Fifteen Thousand Hours*. Wells: Open Books.

Sammons, P., Thomas, S. and Mortimore, P. (1997) *Forging Links: Effective Schools and Effective Departments*. London: Paul Chapman.

Schein, E. (1980) *Organisational Psychology* (3rd edn). Englewood Cliffs, NJ: Prentice-Hall.

Schon, D.A. (1983) *The Reflective Practitioner: How Professionals Think in Action*. London: Temple Books.

Scottish Executive (2000) *The Standards in Scotland's Schools, etc., Act*. Edinburgh: HMSO.

SEED (2001) *A Teaching Profession for the 21st Century. Agreement Reached Following Recommendations Made in the McCrone Report*. Edinburgh: SEED.

Senge, P. (1990) *The Fifth Discipline: The Art and Practice of the Learning*

Organisation. New York: Doubleday.

Senge, P. (1996) The leader's new work: building learning organisations. In K. Starkey (ed.) *How Organisations Learn*. London: International Thomson Business Press.

Simpson, M., Gooday, M. and Payne, F. (2000) *SQH Programme Evaluation: The Role of the Supporter and the Effects on the School of having a Candidate*. Edinburgh: University of Edinburgh and Northern College.

Smith, P. and West-Burnham, T. (eds.) (1993) *Mentoring in the Effective School*. Harlow: Longman.

SOED (1994a) *Higher Still: Opportunity for All*. Edinburgh: The Scottish Office.

SOED (1994b) *5–14; A Practical Guide for Teachers in Primary and Secondary Schools*. Edinburgh: HMSO.

SOEID (1986b) *Proposals for Developing a Framework for Continuing Professional Development for the Teaching Profession in Scotland. Consultation Document*. Edinburgh: SOEID.

SOEID (1996a) *Proposals for Developing a Scottish Qualification for Headship*. Edinburgh: SOEID.

SOEID (1996b) *How Good is Our School – Using Performance Indicators for Self-Evaluation*. Edinburgh: Audit Unit.

SOEID (1998a) *The Standard for Headship in Scotland*. Stirling: SQH Unit.

SOEID (1998b) *Proposals for Developing a Framework for Continuing Professional Development for the Teaching Profession in Scotland. Consultation Document*. Edinburgh: SOEID.

SOEID (1998c) *The Scottish Qualification for Headship: Programme Outline*. Stirling: SQH Unit.

Southworth, G. (1995) *Talking Heads: Voices of Experience: An Investigation in Primary Headship in the 1990s*. Cambridge: Cambridge Institute of Education.

Stenhouse, L. (1975) *An Introduction to Curriculum Research and Development*. London: Heinemann.

Stewart, J. and McGoldrick, J. (eds.) (1996) *Human Resource Development*. London: Pitman Publishing.

Stoll, L. and Fink, D. (1996) *Changing our Schools*. Buckingham: Open University Press.

Summers, A.A. and Wolfe, B.L. (1977) Do schools make a difference? *American Economic Review* 64: 639–52.

Sutherland, S. (1997) *Teacher Education and Training. Report 10 of the Dearing Report*. London: HMSO.

Swanson, R.A. and Richard, A. (1994) *Analysis for Improving Performance: Tools for Diagnosing Organizations and Documenting Workplace Expertise*. San Francisco. Berrett-Koehler.

Talbert, J.E. and McLaughlin, M.W. (1996) Teacher professionalism in local school contexts. In I. Goodson and A. Hargreaves (eds.) *Teachers' Professional Lives*. London: Falmer Press.

Taylor, I. (1997) *Developing Learning in Professional Education: Partnerships for Practice*. Buckingham: Open University Press and the Society for Research into Higher Education.

Thompson, B., Menmuir, J., Forde, C., McCreath, D., Forbes, D. and Verth, J. (1996) *Professional Development through Work Based Learning Agreements*. Glasgow: University of Strathclyde.

Tripp, D. (1993) *Critical Incidents in Teaching: Developing Professional Judgement*. London: Routledge.

Vaill, P.B. (1996) The purposing of high-performing systems. On K. Starkey (ed.) *How Organisations Learn*. London: International Thomson Business Press.

Van Velzen, W. (1985) *Making School Improvement Work – a Conceptual Guide to Practice*. Leuven, Belgium: ACCO.

Vygotsky, L.S.(1962) *Thought and Language*. Cambridge, MA: MIT Press.

Vygotsky, L.S. (1978) *Mind in Society: The Development of Higher Psychological Processes*. Cambridge, MA: Harvard University Press.

Walsh, K. (1995) *Public Services and Market Mechanisms; Competition, Contracting and the New Public Management*. Basingstoke: Macmillan.

Weber, S. and Mitchell, C. (1996) Using drawings to interrogate professional identity and the popular culture of teaching. In I. Goodson and A. Hargreaves (eds.) *Teachers' Professional Lives*. London: Falmer Press.

Weick, K. (1995) *Sense-Making in Organisations*. Thousand Oaks, CA: Sage.

Winstanley, D. and Stuart-Smith, K. (1996) Policing performance: the ethics of performance management. *Personnel Review* 25(6): 66–84.

Winter, R. and Maisch, M. (1996) The 'ASSET' programme: the development of a competence-based honours degree in social work. In D. Hustler and D. MacIntyre (eds.) *Developing Competent Teachers: Approaches to Professional Competence in Teacher Education*. London: David Fulton.

Wragg, E.C. and Conrad, E. (1996) *Teacher Appraisal Observed*. London: Routledge.

Index

absorption, learning, 57
accommodation, learning, 57
accountability
  appraisal, 23
  individual professional, 5–6, 14
  managerial model, WBL, 87
accreditation, 166
achievement, school-based, 52–3
achievement for all, 170
action learning/research cycle, 59
action research
  collaborative, 26
  Lewin's model of, 93
  reflective practice, 66
Advanced Skills Teacher, 35, 91
Advanced Teacher Standards, 31
affiliation, 68, 75–6
appraisal
  accountability, 23
  core competences, 85
  cycle, 4
  disconnecting from pay
    discussions, 49–50
  managerial model, WBL, 84
  performance-related pay, 47
  Scotland, 25
apprenticeship learning, 89
aspiration, 75–6
assessment *see* performance
  assessment
ASSET standards, 9
autonomy
  individuals, improving perfor-
    mance, 6t

teacher isolation and, 71–3

Beacon Schools, 29
behaviourist approach, professional
  improvement, 12–13
beliefs
  and behaviours, 27–8
  process knowledge, 14
Best Value, 18
Better Schools, 26
business, performance management,
  UK, 39–50

capability, 9, 174–5
career rewards, WBL, 84, 90, 94
Centre for Educational Research and
  Innovation, 20
change
  accounting for, in learning, 145–6
  professional practice, 56–78
  staff development as key to, 16
  see also cultural change; social
    change
Chartered Teacher, 25, 33, 91
choice, of schooling, 1
Citizen's Charter, 18
City Academy Status, 55
coaching, 77
cognitive development
  craft/professional model, 92t
  managerial model, 88t
  OD model, 97t
  SQH, 102–3, 112–14
  WBL, 80, 81

cognitive processes, 76
cognitive structures, expertise, 62
cohort networking, 76–7
collaborative culture, learning, 35
collaborative inquiry, 77
commentaries, performance
　　assessment, 155–63
Committee on the In-service Training
　　of Teachers, 31
competence
　　composing claims for, 157–8
　　loss of, 12
competence-based assessment, 149–50
competences
　　appraisal, 85
　　initial teacher education, 28–9, 32
　　management, 115, 133, 154–5
　　public service, 9
competency-based pay, 40
competent performance, 8–9
conformity, mentoring, 91–2
conservatism, mentoring, 91–2
Consortium for Policy Research in
　　Education, 53–4
consultation exercise, CPD, 32–3
continuing professional development,
　　16–17, 25–33
　　different approaches to
　　　implementing, 37
　　impact on practice, 170
　　modifying assumptions and
　　　behaviour, 58
　　strategy document, 34–6, 47
　　work-based learning, 80–1
continuous improvement, 41–2
contracting out, service provision,
　　18–19
core competencies, 85
craft knowledge, 13, 90–1
craft/professional model, WBL, 88–92
creativity, managerial model, WBL, 87
critical friendship, 116
critical reflection, 103
critical review, 42
cultural assumptions, competent
　　performance, 8
cultural change, managerial model,
　　WBL, 84–5

culture of performance management,
　　41–2
curriculum, control of, 25–8

decision-making, involvement of staff,
　　128
delegation, 145–6
Development Programme, (5–14),
　　31–2
development planning, schools, 27,
　　94, 96, 128–9
development projects, SQH, 106
double-loop improvement, 11–12

economic rewards, WBL, 84, 90
Education Act (1986), 21
Education Action Zones, 19, 21, 55
Education Reform Act (1988), 21, 94
effort, associated with change, 58–9
elaborated knowledge, 61
employment profiles, similarity,
　　teachers and business, 40
England
　　national CPD priorities, 30t
　　School Achievement Award, 52–3
　　school improvement, 21–2
environment, interpreting, 60–2
European Foundation for Quality
　　Management, 7
examination results, 43
Excellence in Cities, 21
Excellence in Schools, 34
experiences
　　cognitive development, 113–14
　　influencing change, 59–60
experiential learning
　　craft/professional model, 92t
　　managerial model, 88t
　　OD model, 97t
　　project work, 129–30
　　SQH, 102, 105–9
　　successful, 150–1
　　WBL, 80
expertise, cognitive structures, 62
external influences, 44
extrinsic rewards
　　craft/professional model, 90
　　managerial model, 84

OD model, 94
fair rewards, 46–7
Fast Track scheme, 29
feedback, 41, 129
field assessors, 164–5

General Teaching Council
  (Scotland), 33
goal-setting theory, 4
good practice model, 94
Good Value CPD, 34–5
Graduate Teacher Training
  Schemes, 28–9
grant-maintained schools, 21
group effects, practice, 73–5
Guidelines, (5–14), 22
Guidelines for Review and Internal
  Development, 26

headship, qualifications for, 31
headteachers
  effective, 61
  interpreting self, 62–3
  as lead teachers, 110
  school culture, 73
  as supporters, 138
  see also Leadership Programme for
    Serving Headteachers; National
    Professional Qualification for
    Headship
hierarchical rational model of
  learning, 59
Higher Still, 31–2
human resources management, 85

ICT-based learning, 46
ideas, divide between practice
  and, 113
identity, individuals; responses
  to, 69–70
ideologies, WBL, 109–10
improvement
  achieving, 169–76
  culture of, 95–6
  defining, 10–12
  selecting the means for, 12–15
  see also school improvement
Improving the Quality of Education

For all, 75
in-school support, 115–17
in-service education and
  training, 25–33
individuals
  accounting for self, 68–9
  improving performance of, 23
  managerial model, WBL, 86
  response to identity, 69
  response to learning, 57
  responsibility for performance, 5–7
  rewarding performance, 48–9
induction, in teaching, 72
industry, performance management
  in, 9
Industry in Education report, 39–50
initial teacher education, competences,
  28–9, 32
inspection, of schools, 21, 36
interaction, human, 14
international performance indicators,
  20
International School Improvement
  Project, 20
interpersonal abilities, assessing, 165
interpersonal skills, 45
interpretation, environment and
  practice, 60–4
intrinsic rewards, OD model, 94
Investors in People, 7, 24, 34, 36
isolation, of teachers, 71–3, 174

James Report (1972), 25
job descriptions, professional
  development, 85–6
Joseph, Sir Keith, 17, 23
judgements
  making and valuing, 44–6
  types of professional, 66
  see also sound judgement

knowledge
  development of learners', 141–2
  teacher development, 13
  see also craft knowledge; process
    knowledge
knowledge creation, 65
knowledge-based pay, 50–2

lead teachers, 110
leaders *see* headteachers
Leadership Programme for Serving
  Headteachers, 42, 45
learners
  improving performance, 124–46
  managerial model, WBL, 85
learning
  changing professional practice,
    57–8
  experience of, 127–41
  ICT-based, 46
  improving performance, 13, 14
  nature of, 141–6, 170–1
  processes, linking, 76–8
  putting first, 172–3
  see also reflective learning; social
    learning
learning organisations, 29, 35
learning plans, 114
Lewin, action research model, 93
Licensed Teacher Training Schemes,
  28–9
line management, improving performance, 6t
line managers, WBL, 83
linear model of learning, 59
local authorities, support, SQH, 119,
  121, 122t
local authority coordinators, SQH,
  117, 119
local education authorities
  changing role, 21
  in-service training, 26
local management, of schools, 21
local understandings, performance
  measures, 43

McCrone Inquiry, 16, 25
management competences, 133
Management Competences Scheme,
  115, 154–5
management development, 28, 48
management style, 45, 142
managerial model
  performance management, 4–5
  WBL, 82–8

Maslow, theory of motivation, 93
mentoring
  abandonment in Scotland, 32
  changing professional practice, 77
  craft/professional model, 89, 90,
    91–2
  in-school, 115–17
  initial teacher education, 29
Milestone or Millstone? Performance
  Management in Schools: Reflections on
  the Experiences of Industry, 39
modernisation, 1, 23–5, 33–7
monitoring
  performance management, 4
  school development cycle, 160
motivation
  managerial model, WBL, 84, 87
  Maslow's theory, 93
  professional development, 14

National Board for Professional
  Teaching Standards, 51
National College for School Leader-
  ship, 28
National Commission on Teaching
  and America's Future, 51
National Curriculum, 21, 26–7
National Professional Qualification for
  Headship, 31, 45–6, 167
National Professional Standards
  Framework, 35
National Standards Framework for
  Teachers in England, 9
New Meaning of Educational Change, 56
new public management, 18–19
New Right, 17

objectives, setting, 43
observation, performance assessment,
  153, 154
OFSTED, 8, 23, 30, 36
Organisation for Economic Coopera-
  tion and Development, 20
organisational development model,
  WBL, 92–7
organisational effects, practice, 73–5
organisational gains, feedback on
  performance, 41

organisations
  mentoring, 29
  performance management, 4–5
output-related objectives, 43

pay
  disconnecting discussions and
    appraisal, 49–50
  scales, traditional, 47
  see also performance-related pay
performance
  awards, 52–4
  defining, 7–9, 149–50
  enhancing, 173–5
  improving, learner's view, 124–46
  issues in, 149–52
  problem of, 12
  teachers and school managers, 23–5
performance assessment
  craft/professional model, 90
  managerial model, 83
  OD model, 95
  school-based, 24, 46
  SQH
    background, 148–9
    conclusions, 167–8
    designing a programme, 152–5
    introduction, 147
    portfolios and commentaries,
     155–63
    structural implications, 167
    tensions and dilemmas, 163–6
performance indicators,
  international, 20
performance management, 1–15
  assessment, 167
  business context, UK, 39–50
  defining, 3–7
  establishing the agenda, 17–25
  putting learning first, 172–3
  teacher compensation, USA, 50–2
Performance Management
  Consortia, 45
Performance Management in Schools, 4
performance measures, 7–8
performance-related pay
  emergent US model, 50–2
  industry, UK, 39–40

performance management, 24, 46
School Achievement Awards, 52–3
School-Based Performance Awards,
  53–4
training in appraisal, 47
performance-related progression, 40,
  47, 50
personal gains, feedback on
  performance, 41
personal growth, 14
personal resources, over-reliance on,
  72
planning
  learning opportunities, 114
  performance management, 4
portfolios, 155–63
practice
  divide between ideas, 113
  see also professional practice;
    reflection on practice;
    theory/practice divide
process knowledge, 13, 14, 113, 166
professional development
  affiliation and aspiration, 75–6
  commitment to, Labour, 34
  group and organizational
    effects, 73–5
  isolation and autonomy,
    teachers, 71–3
  motivation, 14
  teacher-learner relationship, 70
professional identity, 144–5
professional judgement, types of, 66
Professional Learning Framework, A, 36
professional methodologies,
  WBL, 88–92
professional model, performance
  management, 5–7
professional practice, 56–78
  current assumptions underpinning,
    170–1
  linking the learning processes, 76–8
  modification of self-concept, 14
  parameters of change, 57–60
  reflective learning process, 64–7
  sense-making processes, 60–4
  social learning process, 67–76
professionalism

boundaries of, 171
engagement in educative
community, 175–6
reflective practice, 65
profit-related pay, 40
project work, 128, 129–30, 131
*Proposals for Developing a Scottish
Qualification for Headship*, 102
propositional knowledge, 13
public services
competences, 9
managerialism, 18
pupil achievement, teacher performance, 43
pupil progress, 43
purchaser/provider relationships, 26

qualifications
for headship, 31
vocational, 84
Qualified Teacher Status, 28

reading, and learning, 134–6
recognition reward, WBL, 84, 90, 94
recruitment of teachers, 36–7
reflection on practice
commentaries, 159–63
craft/professional model, 92t
learning, 136–7
managerial model, 88t
OD model, 97t
SQH, 102, 103–5
WBL, 80
see also self-evaluation
reflective learning, 64–7
reflective practice, 13
regulations, performance reviews, 24
relationships, learners and teachers,
170
resources, SQH, 120–1, 122t
retention, of teachers, 36–7
retrospective claims, assessment,
165–6
reviews, performance management, 4,
24, 25, 26, 36, 42
revolution, learning, 57
rewards
craft/professional model, 89–90

fair, 46–7
individuals or teamwork, 48–9
managerial model, WBL, 84
OD model, 94–5
Ruskin College speech, 17

School Achievement Award, 48, 52–3
school culture, headteachers, 73
school effectiveness research, 19
school improvement
action research, 93–4
educational establishment as
barrier to, 19
Scotland, 22
strategies, 26
in UK, 20
school managers, performance of,
23–5
School Teachers Review Body, 36
school-based assessment, 24, 46
School-Based Performance Awards,
53–4
school-based tutoring, 46
schooling
diversity in choice of, 1
provision and social change, 17
Schools: Building on Success, 34
schools
developing policy and practice,
169–76
development planning, 27, 94, 96,
128–9
environment for social learning,
70–1
implications, WBL, 98–9
performance management in, 19–20
self-evaluation, 21–2, 36
SQH, 109–11
Scotland
appraisal, 25
continuing professional development, 16
INSET and CPD, 31–3
school improvement, 22
Scottish Parliament, policy divergence, 22
Scottish Qualification for Headship
continuous learning process, 42

learners' view, 124–46
  experience of learning, 127–41
  nature of learning, 141–6
partnership, employers and higher
  education, 37–8
performance assessment, 147–68
  developing an approach, 152–5
  issues in, 149–52
  portfolios and commentaries,
    155–63
  structural implications, 167
  tensions and dilemmas, 163–6
professional values, 45
work-based learning, 100–23
  achieving legitimacy, 111–12
  cognitive development, 112–14
  differences between schools,
    109–11
  experiential learning, 105–9
  features of, 100–1
  reflection on practice, 103–5
  resource implications, 120–1,
    122t
  social processes, 114–20
self
  accounting for, 68–9
  interpreting, 62–4
self-concept, reforming practice, 14
self-consistency, 63
self-efficacy, 63
self-enhancement, 63
self-evaluation
  importance of, 167–8
  individual's obligation, 6
  schools, 21–2, 36
  see also reflection on practice
Self-Managing School, The, 19–20
self-monitoring, 6
self-perception, 14
sense-making, 60–4, 68, 130–1
service provision, contracting
  out, 18–19
shadowing, 153
single-loop improvement, 10–11
skills-based pay, 50–2
social change, provision of
  schooling, 17
social constructionism, 67–8

social domain, place of learning, 14
social justice, standards, 9
social learning processes, 67–76
  cognitive processes, 76
  craft/professional model, 92t
  managerial model, 88
  OD model, 97t
  SQH, 103, 114–20
  WBL, 80
socialisation, 68–9
solution processes, 61
sound judgement, 60–1
staff development
  interventions, 81
  key to change, 16
  matching individual and school
    needs, 63–4
staff review and development, 25
staffrooms, social learning, 70
Standard for Chartered Teacher
  programme, 33
Standard for Headship, 103–4, 106,
  130–4, 150, 156
standards
  concern about, 17
  influences on professional, 73
  social justice, 9
  work-based learning, 28–31
  working with SQH, 130–4
Standards and Effectiveness Unit, 27
Stenhouse, Lawrence, 93–4
Strategy for Professional Development,
  A, 2
student learning, model of, 113
success, meaning of, 150–2
supervision, by headteachers, 138
support, and learning, 138–40
support systems, 114–20

tacit knowledge, 90–1
teacher compensation, United States,
  50–2
teacher education institutes, 28
teacher researcher, 34
Teacher Training Agency, 23, 30
Teachers: Meeting the Challenge of
  Change, 23
teachers

isolation and autonomy, 71–3, 174
ownership, professional
  learning, 35–6
performance of, 23–5
performance-related
  progression, 40
recruitment and retention, 36–7
role and status, 3, 12
see also headteachers
teamwork
  rewarding, 48–9
  SQH, 128, 131
technical-rational model, professional
  training, 59, 82
testing, Scottish schools, 22
theoretical learning, 113
theory-making, 65
theory/practice divide, 66–7, 118–19
Threshold Teacher Standards, 31
total quality management, 6–7,
  170
training, 26, 76
Training School status, 29
tutoring, school-based, 46, 77
tutors, SQH, 117, 119

understanding, development of
  learners', 141–2
United Kingdom
  business context, performance
    management, 39–50
  school improvement, 20–2

United States
  knowledge and skills-based
    pay, 50–2
  School-Based Performance
    Awards, 53–4
university tutors, SQH, 117, 119

values
  and behaviours, 27–8
  competence frameworks, 9
  SQH, 45
vocational qualifications, 84

Wales
  national CPD priorities, 30t
  school improvement, 21–2
whole schoolness, 112
work-based learning, 79–99, 174
  CPD strategy, 35
  craft/professional model, 88–92
  existing approaches to, 82
  guidelines on, 36
  implications for schools, 98–9
  managerial model, 82–8
  OD model, 92–7
  professional practice, 77–8
  SQH *see* Scottish Qualification for
    Headship
  standards, 28–31
  structuring, 79–81
workplace affiliation, 68
workplace support, learning, 138–40